Indian Origins
and the
Book of Mormon

Indian Origins *and the* Book of Mormon

Religious Solutions from Columbus to Joseph Smith

Dan Vogel

Signature Books

Copyright 1986 Signature Books, Inc.
All Rights Reserved
Printed in the United States of America

cover illustration from an engraving by
John McGahey, "Joseph Smith Preaching
to the Indians," ca. 1870

Library of Congress Cataloging-in-Publication Data

Vogel, Dan, 1955 -
   Indian Origins and the Book of Mormon.

   Bibliography: p.
   Includes index.
   1. Book of Mormon—Criticism, interpretation, etc.
2. Indians—Origin. 3. Religious thought—United States—History.
I. Title
BX8627.V64   1986   288.3'22   86-61016
ISBN 0-941214-42-7

to my parents

Contents

Preface	1
Introduction	3
Chapter One: The Coming Forth of the Book of Mormon	11
Chapter Two: New World Antiquities	21
Chapter Three: The Origin of the American Indians	35
Chapter Four: Indians and Mound Builders	53
Conclusion	71
Endnotes	75
Bibliography	103
Scriptural References	145
Index	147

Preface

This study involves numerous quotations from seventeenth-, eighteenth-, and nineteenth-century printed sources. These follow the originals except in the following instances: spelling (such as the long "s") has been modernized, and excessive italics (except when used for emphasis) have been omitted. "Sic" and editorial brackets are used infrequently to clarify particularly confusing or distracting areas. Otherwise, capitalization, punctuation, and spelling are reproduced exactly as they occur in the primary sources.

There are a number of churches publishing the Book of Mormon today. The largest of these is the Church of Jesus Christ of Latter-day Saints in Salt Lake City, Utah. Others include the Reorganized Church of Jesus Christ of Latter Day Saints, the Church of Christ (Temple Lot), the Church of Christ with the Elijah Message, all in Independence, Missouri, and the Church of Jesus Christ in the United States of America, based in Monongahela, Pennsylvania. Although changes have been made in the Book of Mormon since 1830—mostly for stylistic reasons—I have used the 1982 edition published by the Church of Jesus Christ of Latter-day Saints. Where significant changes occur, they are noted in the endnotes.

My debt to American and British libraries and institutions is such that I can offer appreciation only in a general way. I would especially like to thank the librarians at California State University at Long Beach for their courteous and prompt assistance in securing books and other materials through interlibrary loan. The library's microfiche, microfilm, and microtext collections proved invaluable, as did materials at the library at the University of California at Irvine. My thanks also to the Library of Congress, the Historical Department of the Church of Jesus Christ of Latter-day Saints, the archives of the Reorganized Church of Jesus Christ of Latter Day Saints, the Utah State Historical Society, the British Museum, and the American Antiquarian Society.

In addition, I am grateful to many individuals. Among those who read early drafts of this work and offered valuable criticisms were Henry Warner Bowden, Francis Jennings, Tom Holm, Richard White, Margaret K. Brady, Brigham Madsen, Marvin S. Hill, Mario S. De Pillis, Neal Salisbury, Alden T. Vaughan, Bernard W. Sheehan,

Ellwood C. Parry III, S. Lyman Tyler, Gustav H. Blanke, Sterling M. McMurrin, Wesley P. Walters, H. Michael Marquardt, George D. Smith, Ronald L. Priddis, and Gary J. Bergera. Their efforts are greatly appreciated. I would especially like to thank Susan Staker for her invaluable help in organizing and editing this work. Although I have enjoyed the kind assistance of many friends and critics, their involvement in no way implies that they agree with my views, and I alone am responsible for errors of fact or interpretation.

Finally, I would like to thank my family and friends who experienced many inconveniences during the research and writing of this book.

Introduction

> I proceed with mine own prophecy, according to my plainness; in the which I know that no man can err . . . I know that they shall be of great worth unto them in the last days; for in that day shall they understand them.
>
> Nephi (2 Ne. 25:7-8)

> For my soul delighteth in plainness; for after this manner doth the Lord God work among the children of men. For the Lord God giveth light unto the understanding; for he speaketh unto men according to their language, unto their understanding.
>
> Nephi (2 Ne. 31:3)

The Book of Mormon presents a number of challenges for serious readers. I have tried to face these squarely in writing this book. Much of what has been written previously was engendered in the crossfire of a debate motivated by reactions to a religion whose foundation rests firmly on the merits of the Book of Mormon. Most members of the Church of Jesus Christ of Latter-day Saints, commonly known as Mormons, and other groups tracing their origins to Joseph Smith, believe that the Book of Mormon is a literal history of the inhabitants of the ancient Americas. Joseph Smith, founder and first prophet of the Mormon church, claimed to have translated the book in the late 1820s from a set of golden plates he found buried in a hill near his home in upstate New York. Thus few careful readers can escape questions about historicity. For example, can the Book of Mormon be substantiated as an actual history of native Americans? Historical issues are of course further compounded by the lack of a tangible record. Joseph said he returned the plates to the angel or spirit who first gave him charge of them after he had finished his translation.

From the beginning many readers of the Book of Mormon doubted such claims. To them the book seemed squarely rooted in the nineteenth century. The famous Reformed Baptist preacher Alexander Campbell, for example, charged in 1831 that Joseph Smith had brought together in the Book of Mormon "every error and almost every truth discussed in New York for the last ten years."[1] In 1834 the Boston-based *Unitarian* magazine echoed Campbell's analysis, claiming that the Book of Mormon "is with some art adapted to the known prejudices of a portion of the community."[2]

However, with the publication of E. D. Howe's anti-Mormon expose *Mormonism Unvailed* in 1834, the discussion narrowed to the theory that Smith and an accomplice, usually Sidney Rigdon, had purloined an unpublished manuscript written by Solomon Spalding, who had died in 1816. The theory of a stolen manuscript appealed to those who assumed Smith was too ignorant to have written the book.[3]

The Spalding theory, which still has its advocates, dominated Mormon and anti-Mormon literature until I. Woodbridge Riley questioned it in his 1902 book, *The Founder of Mormonism: A Psychological Study of Joseph Smith, Jr.* Riley, in effect, went back to exploring the kinds of parallels Campbell had suggested between the nineteenth-century environment and the text of the Book of Mormon, demonstrating a dependence on a more modern world view but not direct borrowings from any other text. The subject was picked up forty years later by Fawn M. Brodie in *No Man Knows My History: The Life of Joseph Smith*. She delivered the fatal blow to the Spalding theory and followed Riley's environmental approach to the Book of Mormon. Since both Riley and Brodie were writing biographies of Joseph Smith, neither explored the Book of Mormon itself in great depth. Some important aspects were missed entirely.

Inspired by Riley and Brodie, others, usually anti-Mormons, have tried to expand and explore evidence which the former writers were only able to treat superficially. James D. Bales's *The Book of Mormon?* (1958) and especially Jerald and Sandra Tanner's *Mormonism: Shadow or Reality?* (1982 revised version) include information not found in Riley or Brodie. However, because of the polemic, one-sided nature of these and similar works, Mormon readers have tended to dismiss their contents as biased and cursory.

Other, less stilted, works have been more concerned with trying to understand and make sense of the Book of Mormon. Gustav H. Blanke's essay, "Early Theories About the Nature and Origin of the Indians, and the Advent of Mormonism," Susan Curtis Mernitz's article, "Palmyra Revisited: A Look at Early Nineteenth-Century America and the Book of Mormon," and Mark Thomas's essay, "Revival Language in the Book of Mormon," have sought to enlarge the scope of approach and interpretation.[4]

These and other works suggest that the literature of pre-1830 America may hold at least part of the key to understanding more fully the Book of Mormon. In other words, historical criticism, which assumes that a work is never intelligible in isolation and must be explored against the intellectual and cultural backdrop of the period during which it appeared, may be a profitable tool for Book of Mormon students. An essential task of historical criticism is to explore various expressions of a particular idea or complex of concerns which appeared prior to or were contemporaneous with the work in question. Such an exploration may not demonstrate direct cause-and-effect relationships but will certainly narrow the field of hypothesis and deduction.

Since the early 1900s, mostly due to the efforts of Mormon scholar and church authority B. H. Roberts, scholars have been increasingly aware of the influence of Joseph Smith's environment on the Book of Mormon. Anachronisms regarding the Book of Mormon's use of biblical material prompted Mormon scholars to reject the nineteenth-century notion that Joseph Smith produced from the plates a "literal" translation. Instead they have advanced the idea that the concepts flowed through Joseph's mind and that he was left to express those concepts in the best language that he could command. Since Joseph, like many in his culture, was familiar with the Bible, Roberts suggested that it was only natural for him to use biblical phraseology in his translation.[5] Thus those who view Joseph as the Book of Mormon's translator have shifted their position from a purely mechanical or literal translation to one which includes Joseph and his environment. Recently Mormon scholar Blake T. Ostler expanded this view to include other early nineteenth-century elements, including Joseph's own inspired additions to the text.[6]

In my own study of the Book of Mormon I have not been primarily concerned with discovering the "sources" of Joseph Smith's thought. Nor have I been interested in tracing links between Joseph Smith and those books he may have read or been exposed to. Rather I have chosen to shift the emphasis of the discussion somewhat, to outline the broad contours of public discussion about the ancient inhabitants of America which had taken place or was taking place by 1830 when the Book of Mormon first appeared. What was the focus and thrust of that discussion? What complex of questions and problems motivated and concerned Joseph Smith's contemporaries? What kinds of responses were displayed by the books and articles written at the time? Finally, I have tried to determine the extent to which the Book of Mormon may have been part of that discussion.

The Book of Mormon itself, I would assert, licenses my approach because it claims to address its modern readers and their problems. As Nephi, a prophet who appears in the early chapters, says, "I know that they [i.e., his prophecies of the future] shall be of great worth unto them in the last days; for in that day shall they understand them" (2 Ne. 25:8). Most early American Freemasons could have guessed, for example, that the Book of Mormon was describing them when they read its condemnation of latter-day "secret combinations" (2 Ne. 26:22; Eth. 8:23-26).[7] Catholics may have winced when they read the Book of Mormon's typically Protestant description of the "great and abominable church . . .

the whore of all the earth" (1 Ne. 13 and 14).[8] And Universalists must have recognized their own beliefs in the "false and vain and foolish doctrines" of those teaching that "God will beat us with a few stripes, and at last we shall be saved in the kingdom of God" (2 Ne. 28:8).[9]

The Book of Mormon invites even more radical comparisons, however. For example, the prophet Moroni refrains from describing the oaths of the Jaredite and Lamanite secret societies because "they are had among all people" (Eth. 8:20). He then warns his latter-day American audience:

> Wherefore, O ye Gentiles, it is wisdom in God that these things should be shown unto you, that thereby ye may repent of your sins, and suffer not that these murderous combinations shall get above you. . . . Wherefore, the Lord commandeth you, when ye shall see these things come among you that ye shall awake to a sense of your awful situation. . . . Wherefore, I, Moroni, am commanded to write these things that evil may be done away. (Eth. 8:23-26)

Moroni is mandating a more fundamental comparison between latter-day and ancient groups than Nephi does when he predicts modern secret societies. Other topics are treated similarly. Nephi foresaw latter-day Universalists, and among the Nephites themselves were those who believed that "all mankind should be saved at the last day" (Al. 1:4). Alma's words to his son Corianton, a believer in universal salvation, must have resonated for early nineteenth- century Christians caught in the emotional debate between orthodoxy and Universalism (Al. 39-42).

My approach takes seriously this Book of Mormon imperative to compare discussions within the book to those taking place when the book first appeared. Making sense of the ongoing religious controversies in both Book of Mormon and nineteenth-century American contexts requires an exploration of the terms in which questions generating the debates were phrased. The same statement may have different meanings when considered within dissimilar environments.

Let me explore an example which will help to clarify this important point. Jonathan Swift mentioned the two moons of Mars in his 1726 *Gulliver's Travels*. At that time the moons were not visible by any means available. But in 1877 the American astronomer Asaph Hall looking through his new, powerful telescope, saw the two moons of Mars as Swift had predicted. Modern readers of Swift have since wondered how he could have made this prediction. Some have even argued that he was divinely inspired. The majority of scientists, however, have maintained that the prediction was only a "very happy guess." Researching the issue more carefully, however, historians Marjorie Nicolson and Nora Mohler discovered that Swift was in fact transmitting an early eighteenth-century notion.[10] Indeed, Kepler and Voltaire had also mentioned the two moons of Mars. On what basis were such conclusions drawn? As it turns out, this belief followed from the supposition that the planets furthest from the sun had the most satellites. Since earth was known to have one satellite, Jupiter, according to Galileo, had four, and Cassini said Saturn had five, it was natural for Swift and others to choose two satellites for Mars—the next highest number for the next planet out from the earth.[11] Knowing the cultural background of the discussion is thus useful in interpreting the significance of Swift's statement. He was neither prescient nor scientifically precocious but had arrived at what turned out to be a correct conclusion based not on science or direct observation but on an early concept of an ordered universe. Still, he could just as easily have been wrong.

A central question to ask about Joseph Smith and the Book of Mormon is: How did this book fit into the ongoing discussion about the origin and nature of ancient American cultures? The discovery of the New World had inspired a whole series of questions and debates. At what time and from what nation did the Indians originate? How and over what route did they travel to the Americas? How did they receive their skin color? Who were the builders of the many mounds and ruined buildings which the early colonists found? These and related questions were variously answered and hotly debated for three centuries prior to the publication of the Book of Mormon.

Archaeology, anthropology, linguistics, and other disciplines were still in their infancy at the time, and scientific answers were yet on the horizon. Although a majority of the early writers came close to modern thinking on several points regarding Indian origins, they did not arrive at their ideas through scientific investigation but rather through philosophical speculation. Some correctly guessed that the Indians had migrated across the Bering Strait and were biologically related to the Tartars or Mongolians of eastern Asia. Such conjectures were based on the observation that the Bering Strait was the point at which the Old and New Worlds were closest and that the Indians seemed to resemble some Asiatics. But, like Swift, they could just as easily have guessed wrong.

In fact a significant minority of religiously motivated people proposed other explanations. For them the subject of Indian origins was a theological conundrum. The very discovery of the New World and its inhabitants touched off a theological debate of no small significance.[12] Who were these Indians? Did they have souls? Were they men and thus descendants of Adam? What was Christian Europe's obligation to them? Were they to be civilized first, or Christianized? Could Christians morally justify seizing Indian lands? These were among the various concerns of Joseph Smith's contemporaries.

In this context Smith's 1842 letter to John Wentworth, editor of the *Chicago Democrat*, is not particularly foreign or unusual. Each of the elements of the letter, as I hope to show—for example, the possible Israelite origin of the Indians, the possible influence of Judaism or even Christianity in ancient America—had been discussed in some form during the ongoing debate. In other words, the compelling questions for Joseph's contemporaries were very similar to those addressed by the Book of Mormon, as outlined to Wentworth:

> In this important and interesting book the history of ancient America is unfolded, from its first settlement by a colony that came from the tower of Babel, at the confusion of languages[,] to the beginning of the fifth century of the Christian era. We are informed by these records that America in ancient times has been inhabited by two distinct races of people. The first were called Jaredites and came directly from the tower of Babel. The second race came directly from the city of Jerusalem, about six hundred years before Christ. They were principally Israelites, of the descendants of Joseph. The Jaredites were destroyed about the time that the Israelites came from Jerusalem, who succeeded them in the inheritance of the country. The principal nation of the second race fell in battle towards the close of the fourth century. The remnant are the Indians that now inhabit this country. This book also tells us that our Savior made his appearance upon this continent after his resurrection, that he planted the gospel here in all its fulness, and richness, and power, and blessing; that they had apostles, prophets, pastors, teachers and evangelists; the same order, the same priesthood, the same ordinances, gifts, powers, and blessing, as was enjoyed on the eastern continent, that the people were cut off in consequence of their transgressions, that the last of their prophets who existed among them was commanded to write an abridgement of their prophesies, history &c., and to hide it up in the earth, and that it should come forth and be united with the Bible for the accomplishment of the purposes of God in the last days.[13]

One further theoretical issue dictated by the discussion in Joseph Smith's day should be mentioned here: only a few early nineteenth-century writers suggested multiple origins for the American Indians. The very term "Indian," as Robert F. Berkhofer, Jr., has pointed out, embodied a unitary concept of the native inhabitants of the Americas invented by Europeans. "By classifying all these many peoples as Indians," writes Berkhofer, "whites categorized the variety of cultures and societies as a single entity for the purposes of description and analysis, thereby neglecting or playing down the social and cultural diversity of Native Americans then—and now—for the convenience of simplified understanding."[14] Samuel Williams expressed in 1794 a typical view when he wrote that "the Indians . . . every where appeared to be the same race, or kind of people."[15] My own discussion of the "Indian" thus ignores the multiplicity of ethnic groups, languages, and lifestyles because most discussions in the nineteenth century and earlier ignored such distinctions. I have tried to note in the following analysis points at which modern knowledge about native Americans differs from misconceptions displayed in the writings of earlier observers. However, readers would do well to keep in mind that I am describing what nineteenth-century Americans thought about the Indians.

The above considerations have shaped the process by which I have weighed and selected the available sources. For the most part I have explored two broad categories of writings: books motivated by theological issues—as is obviously the case with Ethan Smith's *View of the Hebrews* (1823 and 1825)[16]—and those motivated by concerns more antiquarian than religious—such as John Yates's and Joseph Moulton's *History of the State of New York* (1824). I have looked in these sources for arguments, stories, and questions which persisted over time and were thus picked up and repeatedly reworked. I have also explored those sources which reached a broad audience—books reprinted again and again, for example, or excerpted or written about in popular periodicals and newspapers.

I have, of course, tried to include all sources which would have been available in the area where Joseph Smith grew up and later worked. These sources do not prove but merely suggest Joseph's exposure to the subject. Palmyra, where he grew up, was booming in the 1820s. In 1822 a section of the Erie Canal was completed between Rochester and Utica. The canal, which ran through the north end of the village of Palmyra, increased commerce and attracted many people to the area. Historian Horatio Gates Spafford wrote in 1824 that Palmyra "has long been a place of very considerable business, and is the third in rank in this [western] Country, and increasing rapidly."[17] With a population of nearly 4,000, Palmyra had its own newspaper, the *Palmyra Register*, from 1817 to 1823, and the *Wayne Sentinel* thereafter. Palmyra had its own library after 1823, and nearby Manchester had had one since 1817. Several bookstores in Palmyra and vicinity sold a variety of publications at reasonable prices.[18]

Books, of course, were not the only sources of information. Many things can be learned by word of mouth, what Mormon historian B. H. Roberts once called the fund of "common knowledge" inherited by individuals living in the same cultural setting.[19] Joseph Smith certainly inherited some of his attitudes and beliefs about the Indians from his ancestors—many of them leading citizens in New England's Puritan community and members of the Congregational church. His maternal grandfather, Solomon Mack, fought against the Indians in the French and Indian Wars.[20] Moreover, Joseph may have learned about Indian origin problems through popular channels of information such as circuit preachers, traveling lecturers, or community talk circulating in the country store, post office, and other public gathering places.

Working within the context of these theoretical and practical considerations, I have organized the book in the following way. Chapter 1 presents background material about Joseph Smith and the publication of the Book of Mormon. Chapter 2 documents pre-1830 knowledge of ancient American material culture—ruined buildings, temples, pyramids, roads, towers, earthen mounds, and fortifications, for example. Chapter 3 explores the various pre-1830 debates about Indian origins in the New World. Finally, Chapter 4 discusses mound-builder myths and the theory of a lost white-skinned Christian race. The bibliography contains an extensive annotated list of pre-1830 sources dealing with the origin, history, and antiquities of the American Indians as well as some of the sources consulted for this study.

Dan Vogel
March 1986

The Coming Forth of the Book of Mormon

> Whoso shall hide up treasures in the earth shall find them again no more, because of the great curse of the land, save he be a righteous man and shall hide it up unto the Lord.
> Samuel the Lamanite (He. 13:18)

> Behold, I am Moroni. . . . And I am the same who hideth up this record unto the Lord; the plates thereof are of no worth, because of the commandment of the Lord. For he truly saith that no one shall have them to get gain; but the record thereof is of great worth.
> Moroni (Morm. 8:12, 14)

In the autumn of 1830 missionaries from the infant Church of Christ, organized on April 6, launched a mission to the Indian tribes in New York, Ohio, Missouri, and Kansas. Standing in the Kansas wilderness, Oliver Cowdery, second elder of the new church, told the Delaware braves:

> Once the red men were many; they occupied the country from sea to sea— from the rising to the setting sun; the whole land was theirs; the Great Spirit gave it to them. . . .
> Thousands of moons ago, when the red men's forefathers dwelt in peace and possessed this whole land, the Great Spirit talked with them, and revealed His law and His will, and much knowledge to their wise men and prophets. This they wrote in a Book; together with their history, and the things which should befall their children in the latter days. . . .
> This Book, which contained these things, was hid in the earth by Moroni, in a hill called by him, Cumorah, which hill is now in the State of New York, near the village of Palmyra, in Ontario county.[1]

Samuel Smith, brother of church prophet Joseph Smith and the first Mormon missionary, also tried to stir one prospective convert's interest in the Book of Mormon by introducing it as "a history of the origin of the Indians."[2] In fact, the Book of Mormon, which rolled from the press of Egbert B. Grandin of Palmyra, New York, in late March 1830, was but one of many books purporting to reveal the true origin and history of the American Indians.

But this book was different. It did not explain the Indian mystery through natural philosophy or argumentation but rather claimed to be a heavenly-inspired translation of a record engraved on gold plates and deposited anciently in a stone box at the summit of a hill in western New York. By means of a "seer stone" used for divining things unseen to the natural eye, Joseph Smith said he translated the ancient hieroglyphics into English. Joseph was twenty-three years old when the Book of Mormon was published, but his story began several years earlier.

The publication of the Book of Mormon did not occasion the first suspicion of Joseph Smith's claims. Even before the Book of Mormon appeared, young Joseph had gained a local reputation as a "stone-peeper" or "crystal-gazer." By looking into a stone, he claimed to know where treasures were hidden in the earth. And at one time he belonged to a money-digging company which traveled the countryside in search of Spanish and Indian treasure in Palmyra, Manchester, Colesville, South Bainbridge, Harmony, and other places in New York and Pennsylvania.

In October 1825 Josiah Stowell, a well-to-do farmer, traveled from South Bainbridge (now Afton), New York, to the Smith farm in Manchester township to ask the nineteen-year-old Joseph to help him locate a lost Spanish silver mine in the Susquehanna Valley. Lucy Smith, Joseph's mother, records that Stowell came to her son "on account of having heard that he [Smith] possessed certain keys, by which he could discern things invisible to the natural eye."[3] Stowell had previously informed the Smiths about the mine, but Joseph had purportedly warned him that "the treasure must be guarded by some clever spirit."[4] Unsuccessful in his attempt to locate the treasure, Stowell now sought the help of Joseph and his stone.

A money-digging company was formed and a contract drawn up spelling out the terms by which the treasure would be divided among the interested parties.[5] According to Joseph's later recollection, he was paid fourteen dollars a month for his services.[6] After less than a month of discouraging work, the little group of speculators disbanded, although Smith stayed on four additional months in Stowell's employ. According to Smith, he had been successful in locating the treasures, but the diggers were unable to unearth them. The men did not give up easily, however, and followed Smith's directions in attempting to break the spirit's enchantment.

Smith reportedly used various magic devices—animal sacrifice, magic circles, zodiac, and other formulae—in order to win the treasures from their guardian spirits.[7] Although many of the religiously orthodox would have been appalled by such practices, others of the devout participated in folk religion and the occult without such apprehension. Thus Lucy Smith spoke freely of her family's involvement with the "faculty

THE COMING FORTH OF THE BOOK OF MORMON   13

of Abrac," "magic circles," and "sooth saying," adding that such pursuits did not cause them to neglect their other work.[8]

Joseph Smith's stay in South Bainbridge was not without trouble. Peter G. Bridgman, Stowell's nephew, believed Joseph was swindling money from his uncle and swore out a warrant against him as a disorderly person and imposter. According to notes of the 20 March 1826 trial recorded in the docket book of Judge Albert Neely, Joseph testified that he could "determine where hidden treasures in the bowels of the earth were" and that he had been stone-gazing for "three years."[9] Josiah Stowell also took the witness stand and said he "positively knew" Smith possessed the gift of "seeing those valuable treasures through the medium of said stone." Horace Stowell testified that Joseph would look into the stone placed in a hat to exclude light and then claim to see a chest of money buried several miles away. Jonathan Thompson described one money-digging excursion during which Smith said he located an Indian treasure by looking into his stone placed in a hat. However, an enchantment kept the men from obtaining the treasure. Two witnesses, Arad Stowell and a Mr. McMaster, gave the only negative appraisals of Smith's ability with the stone, both claiming that they could see through his tricks. According to the court record, Smith was found guilty of disorderly conduct but apparently, as a first offender, was allowed to escape quietly.[10]

Back in Palmyra, Joseph resumed his money-digging operations. Martin Harris, a prominent member of the community and financial backer of the Book of Mormon, remembered the money diggers:

> There was a company there in that neighborhood, who were digging for money supposed to have been hidden by the ancients. Of this company were old Mr. Stowel—I think his name was Josiah—also old Mr. Beman, also Samuel Lawrence, George Proper, Joseph Smith, jr., and his father, and his brother Hiram Smith. They dug for money in Palmyra, Manchester, also in Pennsylvania, and other places. . . . It was reported by these money diggers, that they had found boxes, but before they could secure them, they would sink into the earth.[11]

In September 1827 Josiah Stowell came to visit the Smiths in Palmyra and to dig for money.[12] Joseph Knight, Sr., Alvah Beaman, a "great rodsman" in his own right, and Samuel Lawrence, a "seer," were also there.[13] It was during this reunion of money diggers that Joseph claimed to have come into possession of the gold plates.

Joseph Smith dictated an account of how he obtained and translated the Indian record as part of a history of the church begun in 1838. Here he drew a distinct line between his earlier money-digging experiences and his discovery of the gold plates. But earlier versions of the story, which can be reconstructed from the accounts of those involved at the time, did not make such a clear distinction.

According to these early accounts, Joseph reported that one night in September 1823 a "spirit" appeared to him three times to tell him of an ancient Indian history engraved on gold plates.[14] The book, the messenger explained, had been deposited (about A.D. 421) in a stone box hidden under a large rock near the summit of a large mound of earth only a few miles south of his father's farm. The following day, Smith reportedly climbed the near-by hill and located the stone box by looking into his seer stone.[15] Using a lever, he pried the large rock away from the ancient vault and gazed in at the gold plates. The accounts differ as to what happened next. However, all agree that Smith encountered difficulty in obtaining the plates. For example, a neighbor, Willard Chase, himself a money digger, learned of the matter from Joseph's father in 1827. He recalled that the elder Smith said Joseph

> took out the book of gold; but fearing some one might discover where he got it, he laid it down to place back the top stone, as he found it; and turning round, to his surprise there was no book in sight. He again opened the box, and in it saw the book, and attempted to take it out, but was hindered. He saw in the box something like a toad, which soon assumed the appearance of a man, and struck him on the side of his head—Not being discouraged at trifles, he again stooped down and strove to take the book, when the spirit struck him again, and knocked him three or four rods, and hurt him prodigiously.[16]

Martin Harris's controversial account closely resembles that of Chase. If authentic, Harris relates the story of the coming forth of the Book of Mormon in words understood by those familiar with money-digging and early nineteenth-century folk magic. Harris's account blurs the distinction between Joseph the money digger and Joseph the prophet and translator of the Book of Mormon. According to Harris, Smith reportedly told him in 1827:

> I found it [the "gold bible"] 4 years ago with my stone but only just got it because of the enchantment[.] the old spirit came to me 3 times in the same dream & says dig up the gold[.] but when I take it up the next morning the spirit transfigured himself from a white salamander in the bottom of the hole & struck me 3 times & held the treasure & would not let me have it because I lay it down to cover over the hole when the spirit says do not lay it down[.][17]

Oliver Cowdery, whom Smith aided in preparing a history of the rise of the church published in 1835, provides yet another version of the story:

> On attempting to take possession of the record a shock was produced upon his system, by an invisible power which deprived him, in a measure, of his natural strength. He desisted for an instant, and made another attempt, but was more sensibly shocked than before . . . he

had heard of the power of enchantment, and a thousand like stories, which held the hidden treasures of the earth, and supposed that physical exertion and personal strength was only necessary to enable him to yet obtain the object of his wish. He therefore made the third attempt with an increased exertion, when his strength failed him more than at either of the former times.[18]

The money-digging and folk magic elements are an integral part of Joseph's attempt to get the plates in the Chase and Harris accounts. In Cowdery's account Joseph struggles to get the plates but has otherwise only heard stories about money-digging and magic. Finally, Joseph's own 1838 account describes no enchantment and no struggle. He simply states: "I made an attempt to take them out, but was forbidden by the messenger."[19] The Harris letter may thus throw some light on how the story of Joseph's first seeing the plates has evolved since the late 1820s.

According to some accounts, the spirit reappeared after Joseph failed to obtain the plates to inform him that he had not followed instructions. Joseph had been told not to let the plates out of his sight until he found a safe place to put them. He also failed to obtain the plates, as he later confessed, because he could not look upon the plates without thinking about their monetary worth.[20] The spirit therefore told him to return to the same spot on the exact day the following year.

Joseph reportedly met with the spirit annually from 1823 to 1827. During this time, Lucy Smith recalled that

> Joseph would occasionally give us some of the most amusing recitals that could be imagined. He would describe the ancient inhabitants of this continent, their dress, mode of travelling, and the animals upon which they rode; their cities, their buildings, with every particular; their mode of warfare; and also their religious worship. This he would do with as much ease, seemingly, as if he had spent his whole life with them.[21]

When Joseph Smith received custody of the plates on 22 September 1827, his money-digging friends believed that they also had rights to the treasure, sacred or not. Harris said, "The money diggers claimed that they had as much right to the plates as Joseph had, as they were in company together. They claimed that Joseph had been traitor, and had appropriated to himself that which belonged to them."[22] This forced Joseph to sever his relationship with his friends. According to Harris, "Joseph said the angel told him he must quit the company of the money-diggers. That there were wicked men among them. He must have no more to do with them. He must not lie, nor swear, nor steal."[23]

Matters worsened in Palmyra after the money diggers made several attempts to take the plates forcibly from Joseph. On one occasion, Lucy Smith later recalled, the money diggers tore up the floor of the cooper's shop near the Smith farm. They had been led to the spot by Sally Chase, sister of Willard, who had "found a green glass, through which she could see many very wonderful things, and among her great discoveries she said that she saw the precise place where 'Joe Smith kept his gold bible hid.' "[24] Conditions eventually became so bad that Joseph moved to Harmony, Pennsylvania, near the home of his father-in-law, Isaac Hale. There he was able to work on the Book of Mormon without much interference.

Joseph apparently used the same method to translate the gold plates that he had used to discover hidden treasures. Harris, who acted as Smith's scribe during the early part of the translation, reportedly said in 1829 that Smith could "interpret" the hieroglyphics "by placing the spectacles in a hat and looking into it."[25] David Whitmer, who was present during the latter part of the translation of the Book of Mormon, published a pamphlet in 1887 in which he described the translation process:

> I will now give you a description of the manner in which the Book of Mormon was translated. Joseph Smith would put the seer stone into a hat, and put his face in the hat, drawing it closely around his face to exclude the light; and in the darkness the spiritual light would shine. A piece of something resembling parchment would appear, and on that appeared the writing. One character at a time would appear, and under it was the interpretation in English. Brother Joseph would read off the English to Oliver Cowdery, who was his principle scribe, and when it was written down and repeated to Brother Joseph to see if it was correct, then it would disappear, and another character with the interpretation would appear. Thus the Book of Mormon was translated by the gift and power of God, and not by any power of man.[26]

Joseph Smith and the money-digging company were not unique; many in New England and New York dug for money. Smith's early belief in seer stones and enchanted treasures was also shared by others. In 1825 the local *Wayne Sentinel* reprinted an article from the *Windsor [Vermont] Journal*, stating that many believed in the "frightful stories of money being hid under the surface of the earth, and enchanted by the Devil or Robert Kidd."[27] The *Wayne Sentinel* that same year reprinted another article from the *Orleans [New York] Advocate*, which reported:

> A few days since was discovered in this town, by the help of a mineral stone, (which becomes transparent when placed in a hat and the light excluded by the face of him who looks into it, provided he is fortune's favorite,) a monstrous potash kettle in the bowels of old mother Earth, filled with the purest bullion. Some attempts have been made to dig it up, but without success. His Satanic Majesty, or some other invisible agent, appears to keep it under marching orders; for no

sooner is it dug on to in one place, than it moves off like "false delusive hope," to another still more remote [place].[28]

In his book *Legends of the West* (1832), James Hall related a story about a money digger named Anderson. According to Hall, Anderson tried to locate a treasure in some hills with his "divining rod" but was prevented from getting possession of the treasure by its guardian spirit.[29] Sarah Josepha Hale in *Traits of American Life* (1835) reported a story which she claimed was based on a late eighteenth-century legend originating from Newport, New Hampshire. According to Hale a Deacon Bascom, one of the area's original settlers, was one night visited three times in a dream by a man clothed in black who told him where to find a silver mine under a large stone. Although the deacon was greatly tempted, he concluded that the dream was inspired by the devil and never uncovered the mine.[30] These and other such stories circulated widely, no doubt inspiring many New Englanders and New Yorkers to search for hidden treasures.

Ancient Indian mounds which dotted the countryside were often targets for those searching for treasures since the Indians had frequently buried valuables with their dead.[31] Even some early Puritan and Pilgrim settlers had become grave robbers, taking articles from mounds and other Indian graves.[32] Ephraim G. Squier remarked in 1851 that most of the burial mounds in western New York "have been excavated, under the impulse of an idle curiosity, or have had their contents scattered by 'money diggers.' "[33]

Only in the post-1830 period do sources explicitly mention the Indian mounds as targets of Joseph Smith's interests. On 2 June 1834, Smith and a small company of Mormons visited an Indian burial mound near the Illinois River. After a skeleton was unearthed, Smith revealed that it belonged to a "white Lamanite" named Zelph who had died during the last struggle of the Nephite nation.[34] In 1838, while traveling through Missouri, Smith again visited some Indian mounds which he believed "were probably erected by the aborigines of the land, to secrete treasures."[35] A few days later, Joseph wrote his brother Hyrum to come and obtain "grate [sic] treasure in the earth."[36]

However, several early accounts make it clear that Smith and the money diggers were interested in Indian treasures. During the 1826 trial, Jonathan Thompson testified that Smith said he could see in his stone the "two Indians who buried the trunk, that a quarrel ensued between them, and one of said Indians was killed by the other, and thrown into the hole beside the trunk, to guard it as he supposed."[37] According to Fayette Lapham's 1830 interview with Joseph Smith, Sr., the younger Smith and Stowell dug for "hidden treasure supposed to have been deposited there [Harmony, Pennsylvania] by the Indians or others."[38]

Harris reported that Joseph and the money diggers hunted for treasures hidden by "the ancients."[39] The mounds would have been the most obvious place to search for Indian treasures.

Joseph Smith was certainly not the first to claim the discovery of a stone box, metal plates, or an Indian book. It was known that the Indians sometimes buried their dead in stone boxes similar to the one described by Joseph Smith. In 1820, for example, the *Archaeologia Americana* reported that human bones had been discovered in some mounds "enclosed in rude stone coffins."[40] A similar stone box, described by John Haywood of Tennessee, was made by placing "four stones standing upright, and so placed in relation to each other, as to form a square or box, which enclosed a skeleton."[41] Stone boxes of various sizes and shapes had reportedly been found in Tennessee, Kentucky, Missouri, Ohio, New York, and other places.[42]

According to various accounts, some of the North American mounds also contained metal plates. Plates constructed by the Indians were usually made of hammered copper or silver and were sometimes etched. Plates made of other metals were most likely of European manufacture. In 1775 Indian trader James Adair described two brass plates and five copper plates found with the Tuccabatches Indians of North America. According to Adair, an Indian informant said "he was told by his forefathers that those plates were given to them by the man we call God; that there had been many more of other shapes, . . . some had writing upon them which were buried with particular men."[43] The Reverend Thaddeus Mason Harris stated in 1805 that "plates of copper have been found in some of the mounds, but they appear to be parts of armour."[44] Orsamus Turner reported that in 1809 a New York farmer ploughed up an "Ancient Record, or Tablet." This plate, according to Turner, was made of copper and "had engraved upon one side of it . . . what would appear to have been some record, or as we may well imagine some brief code of laws."[45] The Philadelphia *Port Folio* reported in 1816 that "thin plates of copper rolled up" were discovered in one mound.[46] In 1823 John Haywood described "human bones of large size" and "two or three plates of brass, with characters inscribed resembling letters" found in one West Virginia mound.[47] In 1883 John Rogan of the Smithsonian Institution's Bureau of Ethnology excavated a mound near Peoria, Illinois, and discovered ten stone boxes, several containing a single skeleton and "a thin copper plate ornamented with stamped figures."[48] Thus the connection of metal plates with stone boxes may have been a natural one.

Perhaps such discoveries of metal plates encouraged the persistent legend of a lost Indian book.[49] The legend, as related by Congregational minister Ethan Smith of Poultney, Vermont, held that the Indians once had "a book which they had for a long time preserved. But having lost the knowledge of reading it, they concluded it would be of no further use to them; and they buried it with an Indian chief."[50] The legend further stated that the Indians "once, away in another country, had the old divine speech, the book of God; they shall at some time have it again, and shall then be happy."[51]

Solomon Spalding (sometimes spelled Spaulding) of Ohio, at one time a Congregational minister, took advantage of the lore of his generation to spin a fanciful romance of ancient America. The romance, written sometime before Spalding's death in 1816 but not published until the late 1800s, pretended to be a translation of an ancient record. In his introduction, Spalding wrote that he found the ancient record in "a small mound of Earth" near the west bank of the Conneaut River in Ohio. On top of the mound was "a flat Stone," which he raised up with a lever. This stone turned out to be a cover to "an artificial cave," about eight feet deep and lined with stones. After descending into the pit, he discovered "an earthan [sic] Box with a cover." Removing its lid, he found that the box contained "twenty eight sheets of parchment . . . written in an eligant [sic] hand with Roman Letters & in the Latin Language . . . [containing] a history of the authors [sic] life & that part of America which extends along the great Lakes & the waters of the Missisippy."[52] Spalding told the story of Roman sailors driven off course by a storm to North America about the time of Constantine. They found the land inhabited by two groups of natives.

Given the currency of such stories, Joseph Smith's own claim that he found a stone box, metal plates, and an Indian record in the hill near his father's farm certainly would have seemed credible to his money-digging friends as well as to others of his contemporaries.

New World Antiquities

And I, Nephi, did build a temple; and I did construct it after the manner of the temple of Solomon. . . . And it came to pass that I, Nephi, did cause my people to be industrious, and to labor with their hands.
Nephi (2 Ne. 5:16-17)

[They] discovered a land which was covered with bones of men, and of beasts, and was also covered with ruins of buildings of every kind, having discovered a land which had been peopled with a people who were as numerous as the hosts of Israel.
Mormon (Mos. 8:8)

[Moroni] did employ his men in preparing for war, yea, and in making fortifications to guard against the Lamanites.
Mormon (Al. 53:7)

By 1830 knowledge of the impressive ruined cities of the Maya of Central America and the Inca of South America was commonplace in the northeastern United States. In addition, the inhabitants of those states were almost daily reminded of the building acumen of the early Indians: the remnants of fortifications as well as burial mounds dotted the area. Since most nineteenth-century Americans did not make distinctions among the various cultures and lifestyles of the native Americans and instead thought of these disparate groups as belonging to one race—the Indian—they also tended to see all of these ruins as coming from one group. What must this group have been like to have engineered such structures? The Book of Mormon tells the story of such a people and provides possible answers to persistent questions about their history.

Early on, writers and explorers interested in Indian origins had begun including descriptions of Peru's awesome buildings. Manasseh ben Israel, a Jew from Amsterdam who assembled writings about America in a book published in England in 1652, mentioned a "vast building" which the Indians said had been built by a white-skinned, bearded people.[1] He included in his report a detailed description of one of these structures:

> Among the great buildings which are there, one was to be seene of a very great pile, which hath a Court 15 fathoms broad; a wall that compasseth it, 2 furlongs high; on one side of the Court is a

Chamber 45 foot long, and 22 broad; and the Court, the Wall, the Pavement, the Chamber, the Roofe of it, the entrance, the posts of the 2 gates of the Chamber, and the entrance, are made only of one stone. . . . The Indians say, that that House is dedicated to the Maker of the World. I conjecture that building to be a Synagogue, built by the Israelites.[2]

English clergyman Thomas Thorowgood and American missionary John Eliot, writing less than a decade later, borrowed heavily from Rabbi Israel. In addition, both men believed that the Peruvians "had their Temples and Priests, and they their chambers there, much after that manner which Solomon built."[3]

One of the first accounts published in the United States detailing Incan antiquities in South America was an 1804 book, *A Concise Extract, from the Sea Journal of William Moulton*. Wrote Moulton:

A mile south from the river and bridge, is the border of an indian city in ruins, which from its appearance is judged to have been more than three, some I have heard say four times as large and populous as the city of New-York. It is enclosed with a spacious ditch or canal, with two walls, and is defended by a castle erected on a conic artificial hill. This hill is raised three hundred feet above the surface of the plain, which overlooks the whole, surrounded by several walls, from whence is a covered way which leads down to he principal palace and bath in the city; the form of the city is ircular and contains large palaces, baths and public walks.

The principal palace and bath is an oblong square of about three undred feet long and one hundred feet broad. . . . Along the eastern side of the city runs the Inca's highway, a road not yet injured by time . . . . It is said to extend through Quito northward, and beyond Lima Southward, the distance between which is 1100 miles.

"Their various structures," concluded Moulton, "not only confirm, but prove that they were ingenious, and had good ideas of, and taste for, architecture [and] fortification."[4]

Six years later clergyman Elijah Parish authored a geography for use in the New England schools. The book included a description of the palace and temple at Cusco, Peru:

Cusco is the most ancient city of Peru, founded by the Incas, for the capital of their empire. . . . The palaces of the Incas in Cusco were spacious and magnificent. Some of the hills were 200 paces long, and 50 or 60 broad. The seams between the stones of which they were built, were closed for ornament with melted silver and gold. . . . The temple of the sun was the richest display of earthly splendor. It was of free-stone, lined with gold.[5]

Reports of Central American ruins were also available. A year after Parish authored his book, a book by famous traveler Alexander von Humboldt, *Political Essay on the Kingdom of New Spain*, appeared simultaneously in London and New York. Humboldt detailed the dimensions of the pyramids of the sun and moon at Teotihuacan, Mexico, as well as other pyramids in Central America, including the pyramid of Cholula. He believed the pyramids dated to the eighth or ninth century A.D. but reported that others held that they were the work of the Olmecs, making them "still more ancient." He also described the "military entrenchment" of Xochicalco:

> It is an insulated hill of 117 metres elevation, surrounded with ditches or trenches, and divided by the hand of man into five terraces covered with masonry. The whole forms a truncated pyramid, of which the four faces are exactly laid down according to the four cardinal points. . . . The platform of this extraordinary monument contains more than 9000 square metres, and exhibits the ruins of a small square ediface, which undoubtedly served for a last retreat to the besieged.[6]

Ethan Smith later included Humboldt's description of the pyramid of Cholula in his book *View of the Hebrews*.[7]

Antonio del Rio's 1822 book, *Description of the Ruins of an Ancient City, Discovered Near Palenque, in the Kingdom of Guatemala*, was another important early source of information about Central America.[8] Published in London, Rio's book was cited two years later in *The History of the State of New York*, by John Yates and Joseph Moulton.[9] In addition, Mark Beaufoy, William Bullock, Domingo Juarros, and John Ranking, all publishing books in London during the 1820s, knew of Rio's book and the Palenque ruins.[10]

Beaufoy also described the pyramids at Teotihuacan, Cholula, and other locations in Central America.[11] Bullock reported that the Mexican antiquities included "the remains of pyramids, castles, fortifications, temples, bridges, houses, . . . [and] towers . . . seven stories high."[12] Juarros described "well defended cities," "magnificent palaces," "fortresses constructed with . . . much art," "buildings of pure ostentation and grandeur," and "the remains of a magnificent building . . . constructed of hewn stone."[13] In 1823 Tennessean John Haywood described Mexican temples, towers, and roads, including an account of a ruin found deep in the jungle.[14] Six years later the *American Monthly Magazine* (Boston) published a detailed description of South, Central, and North American antiquities. According to the periodical, one palace found in Mexico City had "twenty doors of entrance, and one hundred rooms," and many "spacious temples and palaces for the nobility" were found in Peru.[15]

Surprisingly detailed, if not completely accurate, accounts of Central and South American ruins were thus more or less readily available to nineteenth-century Americans. Perhaps more significant, however, were the reports of impressive antiquities closer to home. The eastern portion of North America was dotted with hundreds of artificial earthen mounds, or tumuli as they were often called. The Reverend Thaddeus Mason Harris, who toured the region northwest of the Allegheny Mountains in 1803, wrote:

> The vast mounds and walls of earth, discovered in various parts of this western region have excited the astonishment of all who have seen or heard of them . . . These works are scattered over the whole face of the country. You cannot ride twenty miles in any direction without finding some of the mounds, or vestages of the ramparts.[16]

Ethan Smith reported more than 3,000 tumuli along the Ohio River alone.[17] Based on the number of mounds in eastern North America, one observer, Henry Brackenridge, estimated "that there were 5,000 cities at once full of people. . . . I am perfectly satisfied," he wrote, "that cities similar to those of ancient Mexico, of several hundred thousand souls . . . have existed in this country."[18]

Three general types of mounds were described: temple or altar mounds, believed to have been erected for worship, either as altars or as platforms for temples which had long since deteriorated; burial mounds, believed to contain the bodies of mound builders who had been slain in a terrible battle; and fortification mounds, believed to have been built by mound builders in defense against attack by savages.

On 19 February 1823 western New York's *Palmyra Herald* opined that "many of these fortifications were not forts, but religious temples, or places of public worship."[19] Not unexpectedly, Ethan Smith was also interested in mounds associated with religious worship. According to Smith, the ancient North Americans built not only "walled towns," "forts," and "watch-towers" but also "temples." He compared the temple mounds with the altars or "high places" of ancient Israel.[20] In his 1808 book *The History of America*, Congregational clergyman Jedidiah Morse asserted that many of the large mounds in North America, especially the Grave Creek mound of Ohio, "were intended to serve as bases of temples."[21]

If descriptions of such temples were admittedly speculative, the existence of massive burial mounds was irrefutable. According to Henry Brackenridge, "The barrows, or general receptacles of the dead, . . . are, in fact, to be found in almost every cornfield in the western country."[22] By 1851 Ephraim G. Squier had documented many of the mounds he found scattered throughout his state of New York and published his findings in *Antiquities of the State of New York*. Yet many of these mounds had been discussed publicly some forty years earlier. For example, New York governor DeWitt Clinton described in 1817 a mound near Ridgway, Genesee County, New York, containing piles of skeletons. "They were deposited there by their conquerors," he speculated.[23]

Ohio too was well known for its ancient burial mounds. In 1820 Caleb Atwater, postmaster of Circleville, Ohio, published in the *Archaeologia Americana* his "Description of the Antiquities Discovered in the State of Ohio and Other Western States." In one mound, Atwater reported, was "a great quantity of human bones." Undoubtedly, he speculated, "the remains of those who had been slain in some great and destructive battle. First, because they belonged to persons who had attained their full size; . . . and secondly, they were here in the utmost confusion, as if buried in a hurry." Atwater concluded that his state was "nothing but one vast cemetery of the beings of past ages."[24]

Unitarian clergyman Thaddeus Harris also believed the mounds contained bodies of warriors. "The smaller mounds on the great plains are filled with bones," he wrote, "laid in various directions, in an equal state of decay, and appear to be piled over heaps of slain after some great battle."[25] The *Palmyra Register* for 21 January 1818 stated that the unfortunate mound builders must have been "killed in battle, and hastily buried."[26]

Battle seemed a likely explanation for the burial mounds, no doubt, because many of the mounds in the northeastern United States evidently had been built as fortifications. Although rare, a few of these fortifications were built of stone. Atwater, for example, described two stone-walled fortifications in Ohio, one on Paint Creek near Chillicothe. Of the other stone work, situated in Perry County, he wrote:

> This large stone work contains within its walls forty acres and upwards. The walls, as they are called in popular language, consist of rude fragments of rocks, without any marks of any iron tool upon them. These stones lie in the utmost disorder, and if laid up in a regular wall, would make one seven feet or seven feet six inches in height, and from four to six feet in thickness.[27]

But it was Atwater's description of earthen walled fortifications that was much more typical. Near Newark, Ohio, he wrote,

> is a fort containing about forty acres, within its walls, which are, generally, I should judge, about ten feet in height. Leading into this fort are 8 openings or gateways, about fifteen feet in width; in front of which, is a small mound of earth, in height and thickness resembling the outer wall. . . . These small mounds are about four feet longer than the gateway is in width; . . . These small mounds of earth were probably intended for the defence of the gates, opposite to which they are situated.[28]

Several of the earthen fortifications Atwater described were protected by ditches or trenches. Among the works near Paint Creek, he wrote, "is a circular work, containing between seven and eight acres, whose walls are not now more than ten feet high, surrounded with a ditch." Atwater also described at least one fortification which seemed to have been topped with picketing for added protection. This fort near his home in Circleville, Ohio, had been constructed with two circular walls of earth separated by a deep ditch.

> The round fort was picketed in, if we are to judge from the appearance of the ground on and about the walls. Half way up the outside of the inner wall, is a place distinctly to be seen, where a row of pickets once stood, and where it was placed when this work of defence was originally erected.[29]

Other observers also conjectured that walls of earth had been topped with wooden pickets. For example, Thaddeus Harris, who visited some of the mounds of Ohio in 1803, wrote:

> It is not unlikely, also, that these "fenced cities," were rendered secure by a wooden wall or palisade on the top of the parapet; and that the passages were gate-ways, protected by towers built over them. From one of these to another is about two arrowshots; so that the archers in the towers would be able to defend the whole distance of the wall between them; while those in front could ward off the assailants at the passage.[30]

Solomon Spalding described the fortifications of the ancient mound builders who lived along the Ohio River in his romance novel, written some years before his death in 1816:

> Near every village or city they constructed forts or fortifications. Those were generally of an oval form & of different dimensions according to the number of inhabitants . . . The Ramparts or walls, were formed of dirt which was taken in front of the fort. A deep canal or trench would likewise be formed. . . . In addition to this they inserted a piece of Timber on the top of the Ramparts—These pieces were about seven feet in length from the ground to top which was sharpened.[31]

Such detailed descriptions of local ruins were readily accessible in Joseph Smith's day. DeWitt Clinton, for example, described many fortifications in the vicinity of Joseph Smith's home—works near such cities as Onondaga, Pompey, Manlius, Oxford, Scipio, Jamesville, Ridgway, Canandaigua, and others.[32] Yates and Moulton described many of the same mounds in their history of New York.[33] At the very least, Joseph would have seen, if not visited, many of these mounds. One historian has estimated that there were at least eight mounds within twelve miles of the Smith farm near Palmyra.[34] For example, there was an Indian burial mound in Clifton Springs, a little more than five miles south of the Smith farm.[35] About ten miles away, near Victor, there was not only a mound but an ancient fortification, showing evidence of once being picketed, and some Indian graves.[36] There were three mounds ten miles south in Canandaigua, where the Smiths occasionally conducted business. And east of Canandaigua, on the road to Geneva, was the circular wall of one of New York's most famous ancient fortifications.[37]

Joseph Smith sometimes traveled outside of the Palmyra/Manchester area in pursuit of work and probably would have passed through Geneva, about seventeen miles southeast of the Smith farm, on his way to South Bainbridge.[38] Three fortifications, at least one of which showed evidence of picketing, and one burial mound were near Geneva.[39] When he traveled to Chenango County to dig for money, Joseph passed near mounds in Norwich, Greene, and Oxford.[40] Near Oxford, about fifteen miles north of South Bainbridge, there were many mounds and stone-lined Indian graves.[41] Within Oxford village was another of New York's most famous mounds. After describing the banks of earth and the ditches there, Clinton wrote in 1817, "Probably this work was picketed in, but no remains of any wooden work have been discovered."[42] The *Oxford Gazette* for 19 November 1823 also speculated that it was "most probable" that the circular walls of earth had been "picketed."[43] In St. Lawrence County, where Smith's grandfather Asael Smith and other relatives lived, there were at least nine ancient works. And three of these fortifications were in Potsdam where Smith's uncle Silas Smith lived.[44]

Many early writers explicitly linked the North American mounds with the ruins of Mexico, Central America, and Peru. James Sullivan writing in 1795 asserted that the Ohio mounds and fortifications "must have been raised by the people of Mexico and Peru, because the northern nations never possessed the art."[45] Thaddeus Harris asserted in 1805 that North American burial mounds and fortifications were of "the same structure" of those of the Mexicans.[46] Yates and Moulton also saw the ruins of their own state as part of one great project:

> These remains of art may be viewed as connecting links of a great chain, which extends beyond the confines of our state, and becomes more magnificent and curious as we recede from the northern lakes, pass through Ohio into the great vale of the Mississippi, thence to the Gulf of Mexico, through Texas into New Mexico and South America. In this vast range of more than three thousand miles, these monuments of ancient skill gradually become more remarkable for their number, magnitude, and interesting variety, until we are lost in admiration and astonishment.[47]

In 1824 the *Columbian Historian* described this chain of ruins in much the same way:

An observing eye can easily mark in these works, the progress of their authors, from the lakes to the valley of the Mississippi; thence to the Gulf of Mexico, and round it, through Texas, into New Mexico, and into South America; their increased numbers, as they proceeded, are evident; while the articles found in and near these works, show also the progressive improvement of the arts among those who erected them.[48]

Such descriptions of course imply that all structures were engineered by one group—the mound builders. Many writers speculated that this group originated in the north and then migrated south into Mexico and Peru, building greater and greater mounds. Others believed the group originated in the south and was pushed into North America by savage tribes. The fortifications in the Great Lakes region would thus have been a last desperate effort at defense. In 1829 the *American Monthly Magazine* (Boston) printed a variation on both of these theories: the first settlers had crossed the Bering Strait, migrated to the warmer climates of Mexico and Peru where they built their mighty cities, and only later wandered to the Great Lakes region searching for more fertile lands.[49] Whatever the theory, the northeastern mounds were prime focal points— either the beginning or the end. Western New York was right in the center as one observer would write in the *Ohio Gazetteer*, "The place where they commence, or at least, where they are very remarkable, is in the western part of the state of New York, near the southern shores of lake Ontario."[50]

Observers were interested not only in who might have built the numerous mounds but also in how such engineering feats might have been accomplished. How could the mound builders have built the great pyramids, thrown up the great banks of earth, and dug the deep trenches without the use of metal tools? In 1805 Thaddeus Harris cautioned against assuming size presupposed the use of metal, however.

> It is in vain to conjecture what tools or machines were employed in the construction of these works; but there is no reason to suppose that any of the implements were of iron. . . . Nothing that would answer the purpose of a shovel has ever been discovered.[51]

Still the dearth of examples of metal tools did not stop such conjecture, and Clinton's sentiments were undoubtedly more typical than those of Harris. The fortifications of North America, he wrote, could not "have been constructed without the use of iron or copper."[52] Ethan Smith proposed that the tools had perhaps been "dissolved by rust."[53] He supported his argument by detailing Atwater's discovery in an Ohio mound of what appeared to have been a small sword or a large knife. All that remained was a handle made of elk's horn and some traces of oxide, which was enough to convince Smith that the knife had once had an iron blade.[54]

Occasionally claims surfaced that intact metal objects had been found in the North American mounds, and mound builders were sometimes credited with objects of obvious European manufacture. The *Port Folio* reported in 1819 that one Tennessee mound contained "an iron sword, resembling the sabre of the Persians or Scythians."[55] John Haywood claimed that in addition to clay objects "iron and steel utensils and ornaments have also been found." The Ohio mound builders, he wrote, "had swords of iron and steel, and steel bows, . . . tools also of iron and steel, and chisels with which they neatly sculptured stone, and made engravings upon it."[56] In 1820 Atwater reported in the *Archaeologia Americana* that the mound builders "had some very well manufactured swords and knives of iron, possibly of steel." He also claimed that in Virginia "there was found about half a steel bow, which, when entire, would measure five or six feet."[57] Thaddeus Harris indicated that "plates of copper have been found in some mounds, but they appear to be parts of armour."[58] And Ethan Smith recorded that silver, copper, and iron had been found in the North American mounds.[59]

It is true that North American Indians did hammer copper and silver, but they never achieved the metallurgical sophistication required to make iron or steel, early nineteenth-century beliefs to the contrary.[60] Several who first dug in the mounds were unaware that some of the works they examined dated to post-colonial times. Through careful research, the Smithsonian Institution's Bureau of American Ethnology finally put to rest in the 1880s the idea that the mound builders were expert metallurgists.[61]

Many nineteenth-century observers also miscalculated the ages of the mounds. Thaddeus Harris, who counted the rings on the trees which were found growing on the walls of earth, estimated that the ancient forts "were erected more than a thousand years ago."[62] In 1807 Patrick Gass said the fortifications were "supposed to have been erected more than 1000 years ago."[63] Ethan Smith believed the trees on the walls of earth were of a third growth, the last of more than 400 years, thus making the fortifications more than a thousand years old.[64] Clinton also estimated that the antiquities were "near a thousand years old."[65] However, the group of mounds Clinton visited in Canandaigua was not that old. One of the Canandaigua mounds known as the Sackett Site was examined in 1959 by New York archaeologist William A. Ritchie, who, using carbon dating, estimated the site to date from A.D. 1140 (plus or minus 150 years). The settlement was not destroyed until it was burned on 10 September 1779 by Major General John Sullivan.[66]

On 30 October 1830 the editor of the *Brattleboro Messenger* (Vermont) suggested that the Book of Mormon could have been "designed to explain the ancient fortifications and other things seen at the west."[67] In fact the Book of Mormon does posit answers to the complex of questions about how the ruins which dotted the Americas came to be. It singles out, for example, three centers of settlement which correspond to the three areas of archaeological discovery known commonly in the nineteenth century: first, near the north-western shore of "the land southward" (Al. 22:28); second, on "the narrow neck of land" (Morm. 2-5); and third, in "the land northward" in a region of "large bodies of water and many rivers" (He. 3:4). The Book of Mormon also describes the ruins in these three areas as having been built by a single group of builders whose history resembles that of the mound builders who were supposedly destroyed by the savage ancestors of the Indians.

Mormon writers have traditionally associated these geographic areas with South America, the Isthmus of Panama, and the Great Lakes region.[68] Accordingly, the Nephites landed on the western coast of South America about 589 B.C., founded a civilization, and eventually built the magnificent pyramids and temples found in Peru. Those in Joseph Smith's day who believed that mound-builder culture commenced in the south and progressed northward would not have objected when Joseph explained that Lehi "landed on the continent of South America, in Chili [sic], thirty degrees south latitude" or when the editor of the *Times and Seasons* said Lehi "landed a little south of the Isthmus of Darien [Panama], and improved the country according to the word of the Lord."[69] Later the Nephites spread into "the land northward," discovered the remains of the Jaredites, and built the cities in Central America, Mexico, and the Great Lakes region. The Jaredites, who had migrated from the tower of Babel and inhabited "the land northward" until their destruction shortly after the arrival of the Nephites, had rendered a portion of the land desolate of timber and littered the ground with their bones. Hence the Nephites called the region the "land of Desolation" (Al. 22:30-31; He. 3:3-6; Eth. 7:6). Joseph Smith and other early Mormons referred to North America, especially the prairies, as the "land of Desolation."[70] In 1844 John Taylor, then editor of the church's official *Times and Seasons*, remarked that the Jaredites "probably made the present prairies by extensive cultivation."[71] Many in Joseph's day believed that the prairies were created when the aborigines removed the forests to cultivate their crops.[72]

About A.D. 351 the Lamanites pushed the last of the Nephites out of the land southward (Morm. 2:28-29). For ten years the Nephites fortified the cities on the neck of land against an impending Lamanite attack. Early Mormons, like many of their contemporaries, viewed Panama as part of a larger isthmus which ran from southern Mexico at the Isthmus of Tehuantepec to Panama and thus connected the two large continents.[73] When the two nations again clashed, the Nephites were forced to flee farther north into the Great Lakes region to prepare themselves for a last stand and thus built a string of fortifications. Joseph Smith evidently believed that the many burial mounds in the region contained the bodies of the destroyed Nephites, because on 4 June 1834, during his trip through Illinois with a small company of Mormons, he wrote his wife that he and the others had been "wandering over the plains of the Nephites, recounting occasionally the history of the Book of Mormon, roving over the mounds of that once beloved people of the Lord, picking up their skulls & their bones, as proof of its divine authenticity."[74] The last stand of the Nephites supposedly took place about A.D. 385 and, according to Joseph, in the vicinity of Manchester, New York.[75] This of course fits well with the contemporary belief that the mound builders had been destroyed in the Great Lakes region sometime before the arrival of the Europeans.

The Book of Mormon describes in very general terms the stone buildings, vast palaces, and huge temples located in the southern and central parts of the land. For example, in the city of Nephi, located in the northwestern section of "the land southward," Nephi has his people construct a temple "after the manner of the temple of Solomon save it were not built of so many precious things" (2 Ne. 5:16). Several hundred years later, in the same city, King Noah has the people build "many elegant and spacious buildings" (Mos. 11:8), including "a spacious palace" and "a tower near the temple" (11:9, 12). The city of Nephi, like many other Nephite cities, is surrounded by a wall (22:6; see also Al. 48:8, 62:20-23).

Nephite fortifications are described in much greater detail. These are very similar to those in the eastern United States, though in the Book of Mormon they were also built in the land southward. Thus according to Mormon scholar B. H. Roberts writing in the 1890s, whoever built the Ohio fortifications certainly "knew something of Moroni's system of fortification-building."[76] The Book of Mormon describes, for example, fortifications composed of walls made of earth or stone:

> [Moroni built] small forts, or places of resort; throwing up banks of earth round about to enclose his armies, and also building walls of stone to encircle them about, round about their cities and the borders of their lands (Al. 48:8).

> The Nephites had dug up a ridge of earth round about them, which was so high that the Lamanites could not cast their stones and their arrows at them (Al. 49:4).

It also describes mounds of earth topped with wooden pickets:

> [Moroni commanded his people to] commence in digging up heaps of earth round about all the cities, throughout all the land which was possessed by the Nephites. And upon the top of these ridges of earth he caused that there should be timbers, yea, works of timbers built up to the height of a man, round about the cities. And he caused that upon those works of timbers there should be a frame of pickets built upon the timbers round about; and they were strong and high. And he caused towers to be erected that overlooked those works of pickets, and he caused places of security to be built upon those towers, that the stones and the arrows of the Lamanites could not hurt them. And they were prepared that they could cast stones from the top thereof, according to their pleasure and their strength, and slay him who should attempt to approach near the walls of the city. (Al. 50:1-5)

In addition the book describes mounds of earth topped with wooden pickets and fronted by ditches:

> Moroni, caused that they should commence laboring in digging a ditch round about the land, or the city, Bountiful. And he caused that they should build a breastwork of timbers upon the inner bank of the ditch; and they cast up dirt out of the ditch against the breastwork of timbers. (Al. 53:3-4)

Significantly, the Book of Mormon's description of stone buildings, vast palaces, and huge temples—similar to ruins in Mexico and Peru—tend to be sketchy and obscure, while its description of fortifications, which are similar to those known and described in Joseph Smith's day, are more detailed and elaborate.

The Book of Mormon also describes burial mounds. After one battle, for example, the "dead bodies were heaped up upon the face of the earth, and they were covered with a shallow covering" (Al. 16:11; see also Al. 2:38, 28:11; Eth. 2:15; Morm. 11:6).

Early Mormons proudly pointed to the similarities between Book of Mormon fortifications and North American mounds. Shortly after the Book of Mormon's publication, David Marks visited the Ohio mounds and like many wondered who had built them. When he was told that "the 'Book of Mormon' gave a history of them, and of their authors," he became anxious to get a copy even though he doubted its historicity.[77] In 1834 the *Unitarian* (Boston) reported that the Mormons "suppose the mounds throughout the western states, which have heretofore excited so much curiosity, are the remains of the cities of the Nephites and Lamanites."[78] Edward Strut Abdey wrote in 1835 that "the mounds of earth, which, as they now exist in that part of the country, have given rise to so much interest and speculation, are referred to, by the preachers of the Mormon faith, as proofs of the existence of these theocratic tribes."[79] And Mormon elder Charles Thompson added in an 1841 pamphlet that such similarities were "sufficient to show to the public that the people whose history is contained in the Book of Mormon, are the authors of these works."[80]

Furthermore, early Mormons pointed with equal pride to the book's account of how these structures were constructed. Most contemporary observers felt that the scale of these buildings necessarily implied a knowledge of metallurgy, and the Book of Mormon connected the construction of buildings with the use of metal. "And I did teach my people to build buildings, and to work in all manner of wood, and of iron, and of copper, and of brass, and of steel, and of gold, and of silver, and of precious ores, which were in great abundance," writes Nephi soon after his family lands in the new land (2 Ne. 5:15).

In fact the Book of Mormon's righteous Jaredites and Nephites are described as advanced metallurgists. Nephi possessed in the Old World a bow "made of fine steel" (1 Ne. 16:18). So in the New World he helped his people make swords patterned after the "sword of Laban," a sword described as having a blade of "the most precious steel" (2 Ne. 5:14; 1 Ne. 4:9). With their knowledge of metallurgy, the Nephites made "all manner of tools of every kind to till the ground, and weapons of war" (Jar. 8). When the Nephites discovered the last battle ground of the Jaredites (about 120 B.C.), they found large copper and brass breastplates and swords "cankered with rust" (Mos. 8:10-11). The Jaredites also made "swords out of steel" (Eth. 7:9) and dug metals out of the ground to make both tools and weapons (Eth. 10:23-27).

Thus the Book of Mormon's description of the ancient ruins was congruent with contemporary descriptions of the remnants of an advanced civilization which had once peopled the Americas. Every new discovery of a mound or ruin only strengthened Mormon converts in their conviction that the mighty Nephites and Jaredites once occupied the land. Certainly such ruins stimulated speculation about the origin of ancient American cultures. The pyramids of Mexico and Peru reminded some of Egypt. Others compared the Ohio mounds to the high places of Israel. Still others compared the mounds to those constructed by the Tartars of Asia. Who could have built such mounds? Were they and the Indians of the same race? Who, in fact, were the first settlers of America?

The Origin of American Indians

> Jared came forth with his brother and their families, with some others and their families, from the great tower, at the time the Lord confounded the language of the people, and swore in his wrath that they should be scattered upon all the face of the earth.
> Moroni (Eth. 1:33)

> And now, if the Lord has such great powers, and has wrought so many miracles among the children of men, how is it that he cannot instruct me, that I should build a ship? . . . And it came to pass after we had all gone down into the ship, and had taken with us our provisions and things which had been commanded us, we did put forth into the sea and were driven forth before the wind towards the promised land.
> Nephi (1 Ne. 17:51; 18:8)

> For it sufficeth me to say that we are descendants of Joseph.
> Nephi (1 Ne. 6:2)

William W. Phelps and Parley P. Pratt aptly captured for many of their contemporaries the enthusiasm of early Mormon converts for the book Joseph Smith published in March 1830. "That wonderful conjecture, which left blank as to the origin . . . of the American Indians, was done away by the Book of Mormon," Phelps exclaimed in 1833.[1] And Pratt declared four years later that the Book of Mormon "reveals the origin of the American Indians, which was before a mystery."[2]

The men and women who responded to this book and gathered into Smith's infant church were not the only ones concerned about the origin of the American Indians, however. The very discovery of the Indians in the New World had posed theological problems of considerable significance.

Jedidiah Morse, a Congregational pastor in Charlestown, Massachusetts, summed up the controversy in 1793, writing:

> Those who call in question the authority of the sacred writings say, the Americans are not descendants from Adam, that he was the father of the Asiatics only, and that God created other men to be the patriarchs of the Europeans, Africans and Americans. But this is one among the many weak hypotheses of unbelievers, and is wholly unsupported by history.[3]

Since most of Joseph Smith's contemporaries shared Morse's literal interpretation of the Bible, they were likewise left to wonder how the New World had been populated after the entire earth had been swept clean by the flood at the time of Noah and what the theological status of that New World population was.

Philippus Theophrastus (1493-1541), better known as Paracelsus, a German physician and alchemist, is credited as one of the first to suggest that the New World Indians were not descendants of Adam. He supposedly said, "God could not endure to have the rest of the world empty and so by his admirable wisdom filled the earth with other men."[4]

Public debate over the consequences of such a belief dates to at least the final decade of the sixteenth century. "Impudently [unbelievers] persist in it," wrote Englishman Thomas Nashe in 1593, "that the late discovered Indians are able to shew antiquities thousands [of years] before Adam."[5] Suspected sympathy for such beliefs was part of the stir which brought charges of "atheism" against such men as Sir Walter Raleigh, Thomas Harriot, Matthew Royden, Christopher Marlow, and others in 1592-93.[6] Some, such as Raleigh, did not deserve the accusation, but Marlowe and others did. When Marlowe was formally charged, the first item in the list of his heretical opinions was: "That the Indians and many Authors of antiquity have assuredly written of above 6 thowsande yeers agone, wheras Adam is proved to have lived within 6 thowsand yeares."[7]

In the mid-seventeenth century Isaac de la Peyrere, a Calvinist of Bordeaux, France, wrote the first book-length exploration of the pre-Adamite theory, *A Theological System upon the Presupposition that Men were before Adam* (also *Men before Adam*).[8] In the preface to his first work, La Peyrere described the "world newly discovered" and declared "the men of which, it is probable, did not descend from Adam."[9] He based his supposition on the two accounts of the creation in Genesis. In the beginning, La Peyrere argued, God created the Gentiles; then, at a later time, he created Adam, the first Jew. The Flood was not universal but destroyed only the descendants of Adam in Asia. La Peyrere's arguments were persuasively constructed and gave Christian Europe a tremendous theological jolt. Many books and pamphlets rebutting La Peyrere's postulates immediately appeared.[10]

La Peyrere's position did have its defenders in America. Bernard Romans (c. 1720-84), civil engineer, naturalist, and cartographer, was a captain of artillery sent by the British government to North America in 1757. He traveled extensively among the Indians and in 1775 published a natural history of Florida in which he argued for a separate creation for the Indians. Based on his own observations, he believed the aborigines draw their origin from a different source, than either Europeans, Chinese, Negroes, Moors, Indians [the people of India], or any other different species of the human genus, of which i think there are many species, as well as among most other animals, and that they are not a variety occasioned by a comixture of any of the above species . . .

The above account will perhaps raise a conjecture that i believe the red men are not come from the westward out of the east of Asia; i do not believe it, i am firmly of opinion, that God created an original man and woman in this part of the globe, of different species from any in the other parts.[11]

Henry Home (1696-1782), a Scottish judge of some wealth better known as Lord Kames, had not been to America but shared Romans's opinion. "I venture still further," he wrote in a book which was reprinted in Philadelphia in 1776, "which is, to conjecture, that America has not been peopled from any part of the old world."[12] A blistering response from Samuel Stanhope Smith, a Presbyterian minister and member of the American Philosophical Society of Philadelphia, represented the sentiments of many who were concerned about such arguments: "When ignorance pretends to sneer at revelation, and at opinions held sacred by mankind, it is too contemptible to provoke resentment, or to merit a retaliation in kind."[13]

But of course such opinions did provoke retaliation. Those who wished to preserve a literal interpretation of the biblical story of the Creation and the Flood tried to link the American Indians with some race in the Old World. Romans had argued in his book that such attempts had produced little more than a "confused heap of nonsense and falsehood,"[14] but many became increasingly outspoken about what they considered growing evidence to support the opposing point of view.

In addition to English and French, Spanish writers too were concerned about the theological implications of Indian origins, especially in view of their long contact with the Indians of Mexico and of Central and South America. Francesco Clavigero, a Jesuit who lived in Mexico until 1767, wrote an influential three-volume history of Mexico which was translated into English and published in London in 1787 and in Philadelphia in 1804. He mentions that "those who question the authority of the sacred writings say the Americans derive not their origin from Adam and Noah" and goes on to argue that the Mexican tradition of a flood was proof that the Americans were descendants of Noah.[15] Unfortunately, early writers like Clavigero usually paid little attention to the cultural context from which they took their evidences. Actually, the Aztecs believed the world had been created five times and destroyed four. Each age ended violently through ferocious jaguars, a hurricane, volcanic eruptions, or a flood.[16] Early writers invariably dismissed those elements of any story not corroborating the Bible as inserted corruptions inspired by the devil.

Like Clavigero, Paul Cabrera also cited Indian legends of a flood as evidence that their origins could be traced to the Old World.[17] His confidently titled essay, "Solution of the Grand Historical Problem of the Population of America," was published in 1822 in the same volume with explorer Antonio del Rio's description of the ruins of an ancient city discovered near Palenque, Guatemala. Del Rio was sent to Guatemala by the Spanish government in 1786 to examine whatever ruins he could find. His report, written to Don Jose Estacheria in 1787, inspired Cabrera to write his speculations on Indian origins.[18] Cabrera denounced the pre-Adamite theory because he found that American antiquities such as those discovered by del Rio were so like those of the "Egyptians and other nations" as to prove a "connexion has existed between them and the Americans," thus solving "the grand historical problem of its population."[19] Cabrera reiterated the threat which the pre-Adamite theory posed to traditional Christianity:

> The darkness of this historical question opened the road to an attack upon the impregnable rock of religion. About the middle of the last century, Isaac Peyrere erected his system of the Preadamites . . . [claiming] that all the human race are not the descendants of Adam and Eve, and consequently denies original sin and the principle of our holy catholic religion; producing the population of America as the chief support of this hypothesis, and the ignorance that exists as to the source of its origin.[20]

Cotton Mather, one of the leading Puritan ministers of his day, was among the first colonial Americans to recognize the threat of the pre-Adamite theory to religion. In a discourse he delivered in 1721 to the commissioners of the Society for the Propagation of the Gospel among the American Indians, Mather declared: "Let a foolish Paracelsus and Peyrerius pretend what they will, we are sure that the Americans are of the Noetic Original."[21]

Writers in the United States also pointed to discoveries in Mexico to support their theological positions. Jedidiah Morse in 1793 referred to legends of a flood among Mexican Indians to validate his view "that we ought to seek among the descendants of Noah, for the first peoples of America."[22] And Timothy Dwight, eighth president of Yale College, echoed these and other conclusions in his own book published some twenty years later:

> The several traditions . . . of the inhabitants of Hispaniola, Brazil, and several other countries in South America, concerning the Creation, the Deluge, and the confusion of language, cannot have been inventions of their own. The chances are many millions to one against their agreement in the formation of these traditionary stories. They

are, therefore complete proofs against the hypothesis, that these people were indigenous inhabitants of America. Equally are they proofs, that they sprang from a common stock, and this stock certainly existed in Asia.[23]

No less spirited than the controversy over whether the Indians were descended from pre-Adamites was the secondary debate among proponents of the Old World origin of the Indians about which group had fathered the American aborigines. Even legends and myths were mined for an answer to the question. Hanno of Carthage, according to Greek mythology, sailed through Gibraltar with a fleet of sixty ships and planted colonies along the west coast of Africa around 425 B.C. Some early writers suggested that these sailors might have gone on to settle in America.[24] Welsh legend tells of a prince Madoc ab Owain Gwynedd who tired of the constant warfare in his homeland and sailed off into the Atlantic around A.D. 1170. Reports of a group of Welsh-speaking Indians bolstered the theory that the Madoc colony had reached America.[25] Some early explorers tried to locate the Seven Enchanted Cities of Gold which were believed to have been established by the Seven Portuguese Bishops who had fled to America when the Arabs invaded the Iberian peninsula in medieval times.[26] And there were even those who developed a theory that the Indians originated from Atlantis, the mythical continent described by Plato.[27]

However, many of those reared and educated on the Bible turned to that source as well as to the Apocrypha and Jewish legends to explain the origin of the Indians in America. The dispersion from the tower of Babel was one obvious possibility. The biblical account says the Lord confounded the language of the tower's builders and "scattered them abroad from thence upon the face of all the earth" (Gen. 11:8). For example, English theologian Sir Hamon l'Estrange argued in 1652 that the first settlers of America were descendants of Noah's son Shem who came from the tower.[28] To many apologists, however, the Babel theory seemed inadequate since it did not explain how traces of the Law of Moses and other Jewish practices could be found among the American Indians—a claim increasingly interposed into the debate.

Early writers experimented with several possible Jewish migrations: a flight from Sennacherib about 700 B.C.; navigation during the time of Solomon; or a flight from the Romans at the destruction of Jerusalem around A.D. 70.[29] But the theory which received perhaps the greatest support and captured the popular imagination in Joseph Smith's day was that which asserted that the Indians were the lost ten tribes of Israel. The theory is based on the apocryphal book 2 Esdras (written about A.D. 100), and included in some nineteenth-century editions of the Bible, which mentions the Assyrian captivity of the northern kingdom of Israel around 734 B.C. An angel shows Ezra a vision of a crowd of people, explaining:

> These are the ten tribes, which were carried away, prisoners out of their own land in the time of Osea the king, whom Shalmanaser the king of Assyria led away captive, and he carried them over the waters, and so came they into another land. But they took this counsel among themselves, that they would leave the multitude of the heathen, and go forth into a further country, where never mankind dwelt. . . . For through that country there was a great way to go, namely, of a year and a half: and the same region is called Arsareth. (13:40-41, 45, in KJV)

The whereabouts of the ten tribes always mystified believers.[30] When the Indians were discovered, many clerics believed that the lost ten tribes had finally been located. The theory apparently originated in published form with Joannes Fredericus Lumnius's *De Extremo Dei Judicio et indorum vocatione* (Antwerp, 1567), marking the beginning of a long and tenacious literary tradition.[31]

The tale of a Portuguese Jew named Antonio de Montezinos (or Aaron Levi) who had traveled in South America became the centerpiece of the argument proposing Jewish ancestry for the American Indians. Returning to Amsterdam in late 1644, Montezinos astounded fellow Jews with the declaration that he had found the ten tribes in Peru. According to Montezinos, an Indian named Franciscus, learning that Montezinos was Hebrew, had taken him into the wilderness to meet a group of Jews. This tribe of "unknown people" disclosed to Montezinos that they were of the tribe of Reuben and recited the Hebrew formula: Shemah Israel Adonoy Elohenu Adonay Ehad ("Hear O Israel the Lord Our God the Lord is One"). They also reportedly revealed to him their plan to one day destroy the Spaniards, liberate the Indians, and govern the whole continent.[32]

Montezinos's tale was much retold in Europe to support the existence of the ten tribes in America. His interpretation of the event went unquestioned at the time, although one modern scholar has suggested a more plausible explanation for the group. A significant number of European Jews had immigrated to South America shortly after its discovery. The Spanish Inquisition forced many of these Jews into the wilderness, and Montezinos may have found a group who had hidden themselves from their Spanish persecutors.[33]

Another Jew, Rabbi Manasseh ben Israel from Amsterdam, repeated Montezinos's story in a book published a few years later in 1650 (translated and reprinted in London the same year). He also assembled other evidences to support his belief in the Jewish origin of the Indians such as the purported discovery of Hebrew inscriptions and Jewish synagogues in South America and the similarity between certain Jewish and Indian customs. Manasseh dedicated his book to the English parliament and went personally to England to present his views to them and to Oliver Cromwell. His goal was to have Jews readmitted to England where they had been legally barred since 1290. To argue before the biblically conservative group, Manasseh connected the ten tribe theory to beliefs about biblical prophesy they both shared: the Messiah would not come until the Jews were united with the ten tribes in their homeland.[34] But God had promised to restore the Jews to their homeland only after they had been scattered to all nations.[35] Though the Jews (at least their descendants the Indians) had been found even in America, they were yet absent from England. The scattering could only be completed when they were readmitted. The discovery of the ten tribes in America was a sign that the Messiah's coming was imminent. England could play a very important role in the fulfillment of God's prophecy, Manasseh argued.

Manasseh did not accomplish his immediate goal, but his millennial views regarding the American Indians impressed many English clergymen. One, Thomas Thorowgood, rector of Grimston in Norfolk, published his own book on Indian origins the same year Manasseh's appeared. He included Montezinos's account and marshalled a millennialist argument in support of a private religious goal: the importance of missionary work to the Indians. Ten years later in 1660 Thorowgood teamed up with John Eliot of Massachusetts, the famed "Apostle to the Indians," to write *Jews in America, or Probabilities that those Indians are Judaical, made more probable by some Additionals to the former Conjectures*.[36] Eliot, one of the first in North America to embrace the ten tribe theory, gathered Indian converts into a series of Christian communities. With the help of Thorowgood, he gained financial support from the Puritans in England for his missionary work.

Others in New England shared Eliot's view that the Indians were of Hebrew descent. In 1697 Samuel Sewall, commissioner of the Society for the Propagation of the Gospel in New England, expressed his belief in the ten tribe theory, and in 1788 Puritan Jonathan Edwards the younger compared the language of the Mohican Indians to Hebrew.[37] Roger Williams argued in 1643 that the key to understanding the Indian language was to compare it to Hebrew, and William Penn declared forty years later that he was "ready to believe" that the Indians were "of the stock of the Ten Tribes."[38]

In 1775 an Englishman who had spent forty years among the Indians, trader James Adair, published *The History of the American Indians*, which contained the most thorough defense to date of the Indian-Israelite theory and continued the polemic against writers such as Lord Kames who had championed the pre-Adamite theory.[39] Adair presented twenty-three similarities between the Indians and the Jews, based mostly on his own observations of the Chickasaws and Cherokees. He accurately reported many Indian customs, which makes his book of continuing value to historians, but his interpretations and comparisons are now viewed as naive and strained.[40] Still, many contemporaries found such arguments convincing, and succeeding books on the ten tribes theory almost without exception relied heavily on Adair's account.

In 1816 Elias Boudinot, a member of the U.S. Congress from 1777 to 1784 as well as founder and first president of the American Bible Society, wrote *A Star in the West; or, a Humble Attempt to Discover the Long Lost Ten Tribes of Israel* (Trenton). This book drew heavily on the evidence of Adair and introduced a wide American audience to the theory of Israelite origins.[41] Boudinot's title played off that of a book written by scholar Claudius Buchanan, *A Star in the East*. Buchanan's book, which ran through ten American editions before 1811, had asserted that the ten tribes were located east of Israel in Persia and India.

Ethan Smith, a Congregational clergyman who served as pastor to churches in Massachusetts, New Hampshire, Vermont, and New York, quoted both Adair and Boudinot as well as a variety of American and European sources in his 1823 book *View of the Hebrews; or the Tribes of Israel in America*. He added descriptions of Mexican antiquities and the mounds and fortifications of North America—what Fawn Brodie would later describe as "all the items of three generations of specious scholarship and piecemeal observation on this subject."[42] The first edition of Ethan Smith's book appeared in 1823, but its popularity required a second, expanded edition two years later.

By the time the second edition appeared, dozens of passages from *View of the Hebrews* were appearing in another book, *The Wonders of Nature and Providence, Displayed*, published in New York and written by Josiah Priest, an uneducated harness-maker and peddler of chapbooks.[43] Two prominent members of the state had also been at work on a book exploring Indian origins. John Van Ness Yates, lawyer, secretary of state of New York, and member of the New York Historical Society, and Joseph White Moulton, lawyer and member of the state historical society, had sent out a circular asking for information about the aboriginal and colonial history of New York. The circular appeared in various newspapers around the state including the *Wayne Sentinel*, which was published near Joseph Smith's home in Palmyra, New York. The newspaper reported back to its readers by announcing the publication of the book, *History of the State of New York*, on 20 April 1825: "The traditions and speculations relative to the aborigines are laid down at large . . . The work abounds with historical references, and is evidently a production of great research and industry. It will no doubt be extensively patronised, for no library in the state can be complete without it."[44]

Later that fall the *Wayne Sentinel* published another story about the Indian issue, printing a speech by Mordecai M. Noah, a prominent New York Jew who purchased Grand Island in the Niagara River and there dedicated the city of Ararat as a refuge for oppressed Jews around the world. In the dedicatory speech, Noah proclaimed that the Indians were "in all probability the descendants of the lost tribes of Israel." Noah further remarked that the research of antiquarians showed the Indians to be "the lineal descendants of the Israelites," and added, "My own researches go far to confirm me in the same belief."[45] He invited the Indians to join with their brother Jews on the Island.

Using similar arguments, the following January the *Susquehanna Register*, a newspaper published in Pennsylvania not far from where Joseph Smith would later translate most of the Book of Mormon, reprinted the prospectus for a paper arguing that the Indians with few exceptions are "the literal descendants of Abraham, Isaac, and Jacob."[46]

Based on the availability of such books and speeches, no doubt, Josiah Priest would write in his *American Antiquities* in 1833: "The opinion that the American Indians are descendants of the lost Ten Tribes, is now a popular one, and generally believed."[47] He had good reason to celebrate the popularity of the idea, for the fifth edition of his book (published in 1835) announced that 22,000 copies had been sold in thirty months.

Although the ten tribe theory was a popular one, it was sometimes challenged by those who believed the Indians came from Babel. When Thorowgood published his *Jews in America* in 1650, he was attacked by fellow-theologian Sir Hamon l'Estrange who published two years later *Americans no Jewes, or Improbabilities that the Americans are of that race*.[48] L'Estrange argued that many of the similarities Thorowgood had pointed out were not peculiar to the Jews or to the Indians. Other similarities such as legends of a creation and flood could have been transported by a colony from the tower of Babel.

The debate between the two theories continued into Joseph Smith's day. This is evident from a comment which was made by a reviewer of the 1823 edition of Ethan Smith's *View of the Hebrews*. The review from the *Utica (N.Y.) Christian Repository* suggested that a second edition of Smith's book should separate the Indian traits which are strictly Jewish from those which might be considered patriarchal in order to make the case for Israelite origin stronger.[49]

Few tried to reconcile the two theories, however. Thorowgood, Eliot, and Ethan Smith, for example, were excited by the millennial implications of discovering the ten tribes in the American Indians but were forced to discount the possibility of an earlier migration from Babel, since they based their arguments about the ten tribes on 2 Esdras 13:41, which says the ten tribes traveled to a far country "where never mankind dwelt." Ethan Smith interpreted this passage as a reference to America, "a land where no man dwelt since the flood."[50]

However, writers who did not follow the ten tribe theory and were free from the restriction imposed by the Esdras passage could and did postulate two migrations to ancient America. Congregational clergyman Samuel Mather, for example, in his book *An Attempt to Shew, that America Must Be Known to the Ancients* (Boston, 1773) argued that North America "was probably inhabited not long after the Dispersion of those numerous Families, who were separated in Consequence of the unhappy Affair at Babel."[51] Mather further speculated that a second wave of colonists arrived in ancient America possibly from northern Europe or Asia via the Bering Strait, or perhaps even Phoenicians by ship.[52] In 1823 the *Palmyra Herald* speculated that there were two successive migrations to the New World:

> The first settlers of North America were probably the Asiatics, the descendants of Shem. . . . The Asiatics, at an early period, might easily have crossed the Pacific Ocean, and made settlements in North America. . . . The descendants of Japheth [Europeans] might afterwards cross the Atlantic, and subjugate the Asiatics, or drive them to South America.[53]

Certainly the ten tribes theory and other conjectures about possible Jewish migrations to America were part of the more general attempt to fill that blank to which Mormon convert W. W. Phelps had alluded— "that wonderful conjecture" about the origin of the American Indians.

The debate over Indian origins did not end with a solution to whether the Indians were Adamic or pre-Adamic or whether they had come from Babel or Israel. Those who postulated an Old World origin for the Indians, whatever the theory, had to solve other more specific problems. For example, how and over what route had the Indians traveled to America? Where did they first settle? And what plants and animals were found in the New World? Again, there was no shortage of those willing to speculate about the blanks in New World history.

The mode of travel became the focus of considerable debate. When the dimensions of the New World were finally mapped and it was discovered that the Bering Strait was the point at which the Old and New Worlds were closest, many early writers speculated that it was the place where the first settlers crossed. The Congregational clergyman Jedidiah Morse came close to articulating twentieth-century views when he suggested that the two continents were at one time actually connected by a small "neck of land" which had since been submerged under the ocean.[54] Ethan Smith's theory that the Ten Tribes may have crossed the Bering Strait on ice is also interesting.[55] Still other writers postulated that America's ancient inhabitants crossed the Bering Strait in small canoes. These suggestions, however, were criticised by James McCulloh, curator of the Maryland Academy of Science, who dismissed them as wishful thinking.[56] McCulloh himself proposed that the continent of Atlantis was anciently situated in the Atlantic Ocean and therefore provided a land bridge for people and animals to cross.

A number of critics of the Bering Strait theory pointed out that it would have been impossible for tropical animals to migrate through the arctic zone[57] and instead proposed some kind of transoceanic crossing. In a book published in 1761, *Journal of a Voyage to North-America*, Frenchman Pierre de Charlevoix strongly argued against the pre-Adamite theory, contending that the ancients could have sailed to America from the tower of Babel in a ship like Noah's since they would surely have retained the knowledge of ship building from him.[58] "Who can seriously believe," wrote Charlevoix, "that Noah . . . the builder and pilot of the greatest ship that ever was . . . should not have communicated to those of his descendants who survived him, and by whose means he was to execute the order of the great Creator, to people the universe, I say, who can believe he should not have communicated to them the art of sailing upon an ocean."[59]

The *Palmyra Herald* suggested in 1823 that some Asiatics could have crossed the Pacific Ocean in ancient times and afterwards that some Europeans could have crossed the Atlantic Ocean.[60] Debates about such ocean crossings often turned on questions about navigation. Many argued against migration by sea since the ancients had no knowledge of the mariner's compass.[61] These arguments caused some writers to delay the arrival of the first Americans until Phoenician navigators could make the trip.[62] But the idea that the first settlers of America came by sea was criticized by McCulloh. Even if ancient navigators had reached the New World, he questioned, why would they have brought vicious and useless animals like the wolf and the poisonous snake with them?[63] But for the believer, one might as well ask why Noah had preserved wild and vicious animals. There could be only one answer: Noah followed God's will. That might have also been true for America's first settlers.

Related to the question of how the first ancestors of the Indians traveled to America was the question of where they first settled. Contemporary sources, as discussed in Chapter 2, generally recognized that the ancient ruins formed a chain extending from New York to Peru and became progressively more spectacular at the southern end of the chain. Usually those who believed the mound builders improved as they went postulated that North America was settled first. However, those who believed the first settlers of the New World were highly civilized builders who gradually degenerated and succumbed to Indian attack in North America usually postulated an oceanic crossing into Central or South America.

For example, it has already been shown that Samuel Mather and the *Palmyra Herald* both argued that North America was settled before South America. There were those who argued an opposing view, however. In his book *The History of Louisiana* (London, 1774), Antonoine du Pratz suggested that some Indians might descend from Phoenicians or Carthaginians who had ship-wrecked on the shores of South America.[64] Fifty-five years later, the Boston *American Monthly Magazine* printed a variation on this theme, arguing that the first settlers had crossed the Bering Strait and traveled to the warmer climates of Mexico and Peru before they built their mighty cities. Only later did they migrate to the Great Lakes region seeking more fertile lands.[65] Thus the *American Monthly* explained the first settlements in Central and South America but sidestepped the question of sea travel.

The existence of New World plants and animals with no Old World counterparts was discussed only by careful scholars and was rarely broached in popular essays by the likes of Elias Boudinot or Ethan Smith.[66] In Joseph Smith's day, there was also some confusion about which animals were indigenous to the New World and which had been brought there by the Europeans. Serious scholars in the early nineteenth century knew that oxen, cows, asses, sheep, domesticated goats and swine, and horses had all been imported to America, but most others were unaware of this.[67] For example, the Reverend Solomon Spalding placed horses in his romance novel of the pre-Columbian Indians of North America.[68] Many people also believed that an elephant-like creature had roamed America in the not too distant past. There were many reports, for example, of the discovery of elephant or more precisely mammoth bones in the vicinity of the Great Lakes and the Mississippi Valley.[69] One mammoth skeleton was discovered in New Jersey in the early 1820s and taken to New York's Lyceum of Natural History.[70] Probably the best-known discovery took place in 1801 in New York when Charles W. Peale excavated and reconstructed an entire mammoth skeleton.[71] The mammoth, reportedly 19 feet long and 11 feet 10 inches high, stood for viewing in the "Mammoth Room" of Peale's Museum in Philadelphia.[72]

Indian legends about a great beast hunted by their forefathers caused some early settlers to speculate that the mammoth still existed in the unexplored regions of North America. Samuel Williams, for example, said of the mammoth: "We have the testimony of the Indians that such an animal still exists in the western parts of America."[73] Based on the

Indian stories, Thomas Jefferson had also speculated about the mammoth.[74] Modern folklorists who have studied the Indian legends generally believe that the stories were sometimes descriptions of the moose and at other times mythical rationalizations based on their observations of the fossil bones.[75] Although stories of living mammoths circulated, most believed they had become extinct before the Europeans discovered America. For example, in September 1774, the *Royal American Magazine* wrote that the fact that the mammoth "in America is now extinct, is beyond a doubt. . . . The Indians have a tradition concerning them which is sufficiently romantic, and shews that it must have been long since that they perished."[76] An 1823 article in the *Palmyra Herald* agreed: "What wonderful catastrophe destroyed at once the first inhabitants, with the species of mammoth, is beyond the researches of the best scholar and greatest antiquarian."[77]

Some writers tried to imagine what life might have been like in ancient America with the mammoth. Spalding's romance had the natives using the mammoth ("mammoons") for riding, ploughing, carrying burdens, and drawing timber; its long hair was also used for making clothing.[78] John Ranking, inspired by Indian legends and mammoth remains, wrote a romantic account of thirteenth-century Mongolians who used the mammoth in their conquest of Mexico and Peru.[79]

Without concrete proof, theories about Indian origins multiplied. As early as 1792, Jeremy Belknap, Congregational clergyman and founder of the Massachusetts Historical Society, summarized the various theories and debates:

> Whence was America peopled? For three centuries this has been a subject of debate among the learned; and it is amazing, to see how national prejudice has become involved with philosophical disquisition, in the attempts which have been made to solve the question. The claims of Hanno the Carthaginian, of Madoc the Welchman, to the seven Bishops of Spain, and the ten tribes of Israel, have had their several advocates; and after all, the claim of the six nations is as well founded as any, that their ancestors sprung like trees out of the soil. The true philosopher will treat them all with indifference, and will suspend his judgment till he has better information than any which has yet appeared.[80]

Belknap's plea for "better information" on Indian origins was echoed by other early writers. For example, John Yates and Joseph Moulton wrote in their *History of the State of New York*: "While there are a few remnants of tradition to guide inquiry, and volumes of conjecture to bewilder, not one authentic record remains of even the name of any of those populous and powerful nations."[81] To the frustration of those who asserted the Indians were of Israelitish origin (thus saving the Bible, as they supposed), doubters would simply point to the absence of records. Richard Frame, who worked with William Penn, expressed these sentiments in a poem written in 1692:

> Those that were here before the Sweeds and Fins,
> Were Naked Indians, Clothed with their Skins,
> Which can give no account from whence they came;
> They have no Records for to show the same;
> But I may think, and others may suppose
> What they may be, yet I think few men knows.[82]

Another poem, this one by Nicholas Noyes for Cotton Mather's 1702 book *Magnalia Christi Americana*, echoed: "Conjectur'd once to be of Israel's seed,/But no record appear'd to prove the deed."[83]

Some believed the historical lacunae would never be filled. On 24 July 1829, the *Wayne Sentinel* opined that the "gap in the history of the world, as far as it relates to [the Indians], . . . can never be closed up."[84] The same newspaper quoted Thomas Jefferson as saying that the Indian's origin and ancient history was "consigned to the receptacle of things forever lost upon earth."[85] After reviewing James Buchanan's *Sketches of the History, Manners, and Customs, of the North American Indians* (New York, 1824), the *United States Literary Gazette* expressed the same doubt about solving the Indian mystery by discovering a record:

> The early history of these tribes is probably lost forever. It seems almost unreasonable to hope, that further inquiries into their languages and antiquities should discover distinctly their origin and successive conditions, or that any record should be any where discovered, which would tell them and us whence they came, and through what changes they have passed.[86]

Still others, such as Ethan Smith, continued to hope for the discovery of a record which would finally put an end to all speculation and controversy. "If the Indians are of the tribes of Israel," Smith wrote in 1825, "some decisive evidence of the fact will ere long be exhibited."[87] Smith imagined that the evidence would be some kind of Indian book containing the Hebrew scriptures and believed that he had good reason for this hope. Smith had heard about the discovery in Pittsfield, Massachusetts, of an Indian phylactery containing some Hebrew parchments. Although he was never able to locate the Pittsfield parchments, the legend of a lost Indian book buried with an Indian chief strengthened his hope for such a discovery in the future.[88]

The story of a lost Indian book was a popular one, repeated in various forms by Elias Boudinot, Charles Beatty, Israel Worsley, and others.[89] Not all shared Ethan Smith's belief that such a book would contain the Hebrew scriptures. For example, one reviewer of *View of the Hebrews*

THE ORIGIN OF THE AMERICAN INDIANS

suggested that "the ancestors of the Indians might have had a 'Book,' without being Hebrew."[90] Such remarks bolstered the hope of those who were certain that the eventual discovery of a book would put an end to debate over the authority of the Bible.

Such were the contours of the controversy over Indian origins as they existed by 1830 when the Book of Mormon appeared and in 1833 and 1837 when enthusiastic converts such as W. W. Phelps and Parley P. Pratt declared that the questions had been answered: the blank in Indian history had been filled with the history offered to the world by Joseph Smith. The editor of the *Vermont Patriot and State Gazette* also recognized in 1831 that the Book of Mormon attempted to solve "important historical questions, which have caused many controversial volumes to be written during the last century—viz. Who were the discoverers of America? How this continent originally became peopled?"[91] Certainly the Book of Mormon seems concerned with the same complex of questions which had preoccupied many Christians since the discovery of America. In fact the Book of Mormon offers its own solution to each of the contemporary dilemmas.

The Book of Mormon is first of all concerned with shoring up the Bible—to restore faith in its literal history and its promise of Christian salvation, to prove "to the world that the holy scriptures are true" (D&C 20:11; see also 1 Ne. 13:40). Thus the Book of Mormon makes it clear that God did not create human creatures outside of the family of Adam. The Book of Mormon states that Adam and Eve, after the Fall, "brought forth children; yea, even the family of all the earth" (2 Ne. 2:20). It also proclaims that Christ "cometh into the world that he may save all men if they will hearken unto his voice; for behold, he suffereth the pains of all men, yea, the pains of every living creature, both men, women, and children, who belong to the family of Adam" (2 Ne. 9:21). The Book of Mormon warns latter-day Indians that they "must all stand before the judgment-seat of Christ, yea, every soul who belongs to the whole human family of Adam" (Morm. 3:20).

The Book of Mormon also supports the notion of a universal flood: "After the waters had receded from off the face of this land [America], it became a choice land above all other lands" (Eth. 13:2). The book then explains how life was transplanted to that uninhabited world and in the process forges a reconciliation of the tower of Babel theory and the ten tribe theory. The Book of Mormon proposes two migrations: one from the tower of Babel and a later Jewish migration.

According to the Book of Mormon, the first settlers of America after the Flood were the Jaredites, a group of colonists from the tower of Babel who came at the time of the confusion of languages (Eth. 1:33). The Lord, instead of confounding their language (Eth. 1:34-37), drove them to America, "the promised land" (Eth. 6:12).[92]

The Book of Mormon Jaredites were commanded to depart for "that quarter where there never had man been" (Eth. 2:5).[93] In their preparations for this long journey, the Jaredites in Noah-like fashion gathered their flocks together, "male and female, of every kind" (2:1). Their preparations also included gathering fowl in snares, placing fish in specially prepared vessels, and gathering "seeds of every kind" (2:2-3). According to the Book of Mormon, they also had "deseret, which, by interpretation, is a honey bee" (2:3)[94] and "all manner of cattle, of oxen, and cows, and of sheep, and of swine, and of goats," which are said to be "useful for the food of man" (9:18). They also had "horses," "asses," "elephants," and the unidentified "cureloms" and "cumoms," which are said to be "useful unto man, and more especially the elephants and cureloms and cumoms" (9:19). The Book of Mormon thus reflects a pre-1830 interest in elephants and includes those animals which few in that period would have known were imported animals. The progenitors of these animals were transported to America in eight sea vessels, "tight like unto the ark of Noah" (6:7), which the Lord told them to build. After the vessels were constructed and loaded with the animals, seeds, and other supplies, they set out into the great ocean, riding its current 344 days (6:4-11).[95] Soon after their arrival in "the land northward" or north of "the narrow neck of land" (presumably the Isthmus of Panama), they "began to spread upon the face of the land, and to multiply and to till the earth; and they did wax strong in the land" (6:18; Al. 22:30; Mos. 8:8). Life was thus transplanted to the New World which had been swept clean by the Flood.

There was some confusion among tower of Babel theorists as to which of Noah's sons the first settlers of America descended from. Although the Book of Mormon itself is silent on the matter, there are indications that Ham might have been intended. According to the Book of Mormon, the Jaredites departed from Babel and went to the Valley of Nimrod where they prepared for their long journey to the New World (Eth. 1-2). The Bible says that Babel was founded by Nimrod, a descendant of Ham (Gen. 10:8, 10). Many in Joseph Smith's day connected the cursedness of Ham (Gen. 9:20-27) with the curse of Cain (4:9-15), as did Joseph himself (Abr. 1:21-27). This connection may explain why the Jaredites are said to have brought with them some records containing oaths which had been handed down from Cain (Eth. 8:9, 15). In fact, some early Mormons seem to have believed the Jaredites were Hamites.[96]

Most of the Book of Mormon is devoted to the story of a second migration by an Israelite group descended from the house of Joseph. The ten tribes, the Book of Mormon suggests, are yet in an unknown region of the earth (3 Ne. 16:1-3; 17:4). The book thus sets aside the persistent debate about that mysterious group and refuses to speculate

THE ORIGIN OF THE AMERICAN INDIANS

on a solution to the mystery, although the book suggests that Christ visited the ten tribes just as he did Jewish descendants in America. The story of this second Book of Mormon migration begins in Jerusalem "in the commencement of the first year of the reign of Zedekiah, king of Judah" (1 Ne. 1:4). This was the first year of Zedekiah's eleven-year reign, which preceded the fall and captivity of Jerusalem by Babylonian invaders about 586 B.C. According to the Book of Mormon, Jerusalem had rejected the Lord's prophets, including one named Lehi. Although Lehi's ministry is not mentioned in the Bible, he is the chief figure in the Book of Mormon's migration story. The Lord warned Lehi in a dream about Jerusalem's eventual fall and commanded him to flee into the wilderness with his family and others. When they arrived at the shore of the great Indian Ocean, they built a ship which was constructed "after the manner which the Lord had shown . . . not after the manner of men" (18:1-2).

Like many of those who speculated on Indian origins in Joseph Smith's day, Lehi's sons debated among themselves whether such a long sea voyage was possible. Faithful Nephi was challenged by his skeptical brothers: "And when my brethren saw that I was about to build a ship, they began to murmur against me, saying: Our brother is a fool, for he thinketh that he can build a ship; yea, and he also thinketh that he can cross these great waters" (1 Ne. 17:17). Nephi responded by reminding his brothers of the miracles which had accompanied the Israelite exodus from Egypt. He then asked them rhetorically: "If the Lord has such great power, and has wrought so many miracles among the children of men, how is it that he cannot instruct me, that I should build a ship?" (17:51)

Although the mariner's compass had not yet been invented, the Lord provided Lehi with a compass-like instrument, described as "a round [brass] ball of curious workmanship." Inside the ball were "two spindles," one of which "pointed the way whither we should go into the wilderness" (1 Ne. 16:10). The Jaredite colony had simply drifted on the ocean's current, but the Lehi colony had use of both sail and rudder and thus a compass or some kind of directional device was imperative (18:9-22). After a long sea voyage, Lehi's colony landed on the western shore of "the land southward," apparently the Book of Mormon's term for South America (Al. 22:28, 32).

For most Americans today, Indian origins in the New World are no longer a theological problem. The controversies which caused so much excitement and speculation in Joseph Smith's day no longer trouble scholars. It is now generally accepted that the American Indians are of Mongolian extraction, representing several different physical types probably originating in northern, central, and eastern Asia. They are thought to have migrated across the Bering Strait sometime between

12,000 and 30,000 years ago. The biological linkage of the Indians to Asia is based on common features such as the characteristic eyefold, the pigmented spot which appears at the base of the spine of infants, and the shovel shape of the incisor. These traits have been found in varying proportions among every Indian group studied.[97]

Indians and Mound Builders

[The Lamanites] were led by their evil nature that they became wild, and ferocious, and a blood-thirsty people, full of idolatry and filthiness; feeding upon beasts of prey; dwelling in tents, and wandering about in the wilderness with a short skin girdle about their loins and their heads shaven; and their skill was in the bow, and in the cimeter, and the ax. And many of them did eat nothing save it was raw meat; and they were continually seeking to destroy us.
                                                    Enos (Enos 20)

I beheld and saw that the seed of my brethren [the Lamanites] did contend against my seed, according to the word of the angel; and because of the pride of my seed, and the temptations of the devil, I beheld that the seed of my brethren did overpower the people of my seed.
                                                    Nephi (1 Ne. 12:19)

Behold, I perceive that this very people, the Nephites, according to the spirit of revelation which is in me, in four hundred years from the time that Jesus Christ shall manifest himself unto them, shall dwindle in unbelief. Yea, and then shall they see wars and pestilences, yea, famines and bloodshed, even until the people of Nephi shall become extinct.
                                                    Alma (Al. 45:10-11)

The discovery of the New World and its native inhabitants challenged literalistic beliefs in the Bible and promoted a lively debate over Indian origins. But this was not the only religious controversy which turned on the history of the Indians. Another persistent discussion explored the Christian imperative to evangelize. How agressively should missionary work be pursued among the Indians? Could the Indians become civilized Christians? Or were they by nature incapable of such conversion? The context for this second debate was further complicated because political and economic imperatives sometimes clashed with religious ones. Given the complexity of the situation, it is not surprising that Americans held ambivalent and sometimes contradictory opinions about the Indian.

The Puritans of New England came to hold the harshest estimation of the Indians. The French Jesuits who first ventured to North America believed the Indians were "men of nature" lacking only Christianity.

The Jesuits were cultural primitivists who believed men were happiest in their primitive or "natural" state. Consequently, they saw the Indian as the "noble savage" who had escaped the vices and corruptions of European civilization. Seventeenth-century Europe was at first greatly influenced by the Jesuit's optimistic appraisal of the natives of America.[1] Even Puritan descriptions of the Indians were initially influenced by such charitable sentiments. The Indians may have been perceived by the Puritans as uncivilized by European standards, but they were a good-hearted and hospitable people. The early colonists felt indebted to the Indians for helping them survive those first harsh New England winters. Any Indian weaknesses, the Puritans confidently believed, would be corrected by civilization and conversion to Christianity.[2] The Puritans—philosophically poles apart from the Jesuits—were Calvinists and anti-primitivists who not only believed that civilization was superior to the "natural" or primitive state but also that Christian salvation was linked to civilization. When problems with the Indians began, Puritan accounts became increasingly harsh and pessimistic.

The Puritans were particularly critical of Indian religion. The Indians' reluctance to embrace both civilization and Christianity indicated the extent of the devil's hold on them. In his 1702 *Magnalia Christi Americana*, Cotton Mather declared that the Indians were "doleful creatures" and "the veriest ruins of mankind, which are to be found any where upon the face of the earth."[3] "Though we know not when or how these Indians first became inhabitants of this mighty continent," he wrote, "yet we may guess that probably the devil decoyed those miserable salvages hither, in hopes that the gospel of the Lord Jesus Christ would never come here to destroy or disturb his absolute empire over them."[4] In another work, *India Christiana*, Mather concluded that their way of life was "lamentably Barbarous" and their religion "beyond all Expression Dark."[5] Even Roger Williams, otherwise a defender of Indian rights, was appalled by their "hideous worships of creatures and devils."[6]

For the Puritans, the worst charge that could be brought against Indian religion was that of idolatry and human sacrifice.[7] Descriptions of native idolatry and human sacrifice came from several sources. James Adair had reported that "the Spanish writers acknowledge that the Mexicans brought their human sacrifices from the opposite sea; and did not offer up any of their own people: so that this was but the same as our North American Indians still practice, when they devote their captives to death."[8] In his history of Mexico, Francesco Clavigero wrote that Central American Indians "sacrificed men to their gods, women to their godesses, and children to some other diminutive deities."[9] Other early observers described a Mexican statue of a "horrible deity, before whom tens of thousands of human victims had been sacrificed" and remarked that the ancient Mexican people "delighted to see the palpitating heart of human victims offered up to gigantic and monstrous idols."[10]

The Europeans were also appalled by alcohol abuse, a European product highly valued by the Indians. Paradoxically the Indians were being destroyed by contact with civilization rather than improved.[11] "Our vices have destroyed them more than our swords," wrote one contemporary.[12] "By mixing with us," reported *Niles' Weekly Register* in 1818, "[the Indians] imbibed all our vices, without emulating our virtues—and our intercourse with them is decisively disadvantageous to them."[13] A 1786 account in the *Columbian Magazine* published in Philadelphia attempted to counter the optimistic accounts of the Indians published in Europe:

> It has become fashionable of late years for the philosophers of Europe to celebrate the virtues of the savages of America. Whether the design of their encomiums was to expose christianity, and depreciate the advantages of civilization, I know not; but they have evidently had those effects upon the minds of weak people.

The list of vices included uncleanness, nastiness, drunkenness, gluttony, treachery, idleness, and theft.[14]

The Puritans were carefully tallying the consequences of these vices, especially that of idleness.[15] Edmund Burke, for example, said that after the hunting season was over, the Indians "pass the rest of their time in an entire indolence. They sleep half the day in their huts, [and] they loiter and jest among their friends."[16] Hardworking Puritans were appalled that the Indians were not making good use of all of their land. Citing such sloth, they declared *vacuum domicilium* so that any land not occupied or being used could be seized.[17] John Cotton, a leader in the Puritan community, explained the principle:

> Where there is a vacant place, there is liberty for the Son of Adam or Noah to come and inhabit, though they neither buy it, nor ask their leaves. . . . In a vacant Soyle, he that taketh possession of it, and bestoweth culture and husbandry upon it, his Right it is. And the ground of this is, from the Grand Charter given to Adam and his Posterity in Paradise, Gen. 1. 28. Multiply, and replenish the earth, and subdue it.[18]

When the Indians resisted colonial expansion and war broke out, Puritan epithets became even harsher. Instead of "noble savages," the Indians became "savage warriors."[19] It was no longer a matter of saving the Indian for civilization but rather of saving civilization from the Indian. The Fourth of July toast of a group of officers in 1779 was, according to historian Roy Harvey Pearce, a truism of the American frontier:

"Civilization or death to all American Savages."[20] In such a context, the Indians were seen as inherently savage and entirely incapable of civilization.[21] Mistreatment of the Indians became easy to justify.

Given the generally poor image of the Indians common by the beginning of the nineteenth century, attempts by Ethan Smith and others to identify them with the lost ten tribes of Israel have been described by one historian as "part of a last-moment revivalist effort to find a secure place for the Indian in a civilized, Christian world."[22] The ten tribe theorists tried to mitigate the view that the Indians were inherently savage. "The Indians are not Savages, they are wild and savage in their habits, but possess great vigor of intellect and native talent," proclaimed Mordecai Noah in his 1825 speech on Indian origins. "They are a brave and eloquent people."[23]

Ethan Smith shared Noah's sentiments. "Yet it is a fact that there are many excellent traits in their original character . . . such as might have been expected from the descendants of the ancient Israel of God," he wrote.[24] Indians had in fact become cruel because of the mistreatment of unprincipled whites, nor was it fair to judge the Indians by what they did in war. "Their doleful cruelties to their prisoners of war, was a religious custom among them, which they performed with savage firmness; as was their pursuit and slaughter of one who had killed a relative," he argued. "Aside from these cruelties of principle, the Indians are faithful and kind."[25] Certainly, Smith concluded, the Indians "have deserved better treatment then [sic] they received from the whites."[26] He pleaded with his fellow Americans: "Let them not become extinct before your eyes; let them no longer roam in savage barbarism and death!"[27]

By associating the Indians with the ten tribes of Israel, Ethan Smith hoped to stop the Indian's destruction and place a burden of responsibility on America for their conversion.

> This duty of christianizing the natives of our land, even be they from whatever origin, is enforced from every evangelical consideration. . . . If our natives be indeed from the tribes of Israel, American Christians may well feel, that one great object of their inheritance here, is, that they may have a primary agency in restoring those "lost sheep of the house of Israel."[28]

His advice to the missionaries:

> You received that book [the Bible] from the seed of Abraham. All your volume of salvation was written by the sons of Jacob. . . . Remember then your debt of gratitude to God's ancient people for the word of life. Restore it to them, and thus double your own rich inheritance in its blessings. Learn them to read the book of grace. Learn them its history and their own. Teach them the story of their ancestors;

the economy of Abraham, Isaac and Jacob. . . . Teach them their ancient history; their former blessings; their being cast away; the occasion of it, and the promises of their return.[29]

Ethan Smith defended the Indians against harsh judgments about their character and abilities by linking them with the lost tribes of Israel. Following the pattern established in ancient Israel, these Jewish braves had lapsed into apostasy and idolatry. Far from being heathens or devil worshipers, they had practiced a religion with many Judeo-Christian elements. Those writers who speculated that the Indians were of Hebrew descent, such as James Adair, Elias Boudinot, Ethan Smith, and earlier writers such as Manasseh ben Israel, Thomas Thorowgood, and John Eliot, tried to document cultural, religious, and language similarities between the Indians and the ancient Israelites. More often than not, however, such comparisons were based on superficial similarities which ignored more profound differences.

James Adair, who published *The History of the American Indians* in London in 1775, explored twenty-three parallels between Hebrew and Indian culture, including their division into tribes and worship of Jehovah; their notions of theocracy and their belief in the ministration of angels; their language and dialects; their manner of reckoning time; their prophets and high priests; their festivals, feasts, and religious rites; their daily sacrifices; their ablutions and anointings; their laws of uncleanness and their abstinence from unclean things; their marriage, divorce, and punishment for adultery; their cities of refuge; their purification and ceremonies before war; their ornaments; their manner of curing the sick; their burial of and mourning for the dead; their raising seed to a deceased brother; and their choice of names adapted to their circumstances and the times. Both Elias Boudinot and Ethan Smith based many of their arguments on the evidence provided by Adair.

Adair was not universally believed, however. Historian Samuel G. Drake declared in 1841 that Adair "tormented every custom and usage into a like one of the Jews, and almost every word in their language became a Hebrew one of the same meaning."[30] In a speech delivered before the New York Historical Society in 1819, Samuel Jarvis cautioned that attempts to link the American Indians with some group in the Old World "led to many misrepresentations of the religious rites of its inhabitants; and affinities were discovered which existed no where but in the fancy of the inventor." Jarvis specifically referred to Adair (and parenthetically to Boudinot):

> An hypothesis has somewhat extensively prevailed, which exalts the religion of the Indians as much above its proper level, as Volney has debased it below:

I mean that which supposes them to be the descendants of the ten tribes of Israel. This theory so possessed the mind of Adair, that, although he had the greatest opportunities of obtaining knowledge, his book is, comparatively, of little use. We are constantly led to suspect the fidelity of his statements, because his judgment had lost its equipose, and he saw every thing through a discoloured medium. I feel myself bound to notice this hypothesis the more, because it has lately been revived and brought before the public, by a venerable member of this society [i.e., Elias Boudinot].[31]

Alexander von Humboldt also cautioned about distortions which could result from another kind of enthusiasm:

The introduction of christianity has produced almost no other effect on the Indians of Mexico than to substitute new ceremonies, the symbols of a gentle and humane religion, to the ceremonies of a sanguinary worship. . . . In such a complicated mythology as that of the Mexicans, it was easy to find out an affinity between the divinities of Aztlan and the divinity of the east. . . . At that period christianity was confounded with the Mexican mythology: the Holy Ghost is identified with the sacred eagle of the Aztecs. The missionaries not only tolerated, they even favoured to a certain extent, this amalgamation of ideas, by means of which the christian worship was more easily introduced among the natives. They persuaded them that the gospel had, in very remote times, been already preached in America.[32]

But such voices of caution were largely ignored. Many people in Joseph Smith's day believed the Indians were in fact living a corrupt form of the "law of Moses."[33] Observers found evidence that the Indians were familiar with other Jewish traditions as well. Ethan Smith, for example, felt that the Indians may even have possessed the Old Testament scriptures anciently.[34] Others found evidence that the Indians had traditions of the Creation,[35] the Fall,[36] Cain's murder of Abel,[37] the Flood,[38] and the tower of Babel.[39]

Observers were also interested in the origin of Indian languages, the sounds of which were often compared to Hebrew. Some compiled lists of words which seemed similar in sound or meaning. Adair claimed, for example, that the Indians called upon "Yo-He-Wah" (the Hebrew Yahweh).[40] One of the earliest studies which identified the Indian's language with Hebrew was Roger Williams's *A Key into the Language of America* (London, 1643). William Penn also compared the Indian's "narrow" and "lofty" language to Hebrew,[41] as did Jonathan Edwards in his *Observations on the Language of the Mahhekaneew Indians* published in 1788. Adair, Boudinot, and Ethan Smith all cited the similarity between Indian languages and Hebrew as proof that the Indians were of Hebraic origin.[42] Indian writing, however, observed in North

American pictographic rock paintings, Mexican codices, and Mayan glyphs, was often compared to Egyptian rather than Hebrew.[43]

Nineteenth-century observers went even further in discovering parallels. Many argued that traces of both Christianity and Judaism could be found among the Indians before the Europeans came to America. "The gospel had in very remote times, been already preached in America," wrote Ethan Smith. "It is a noted fact that there is a far greater analogy between much of the religion of the Indians, and Christianity, than between that of any other heathen nation on earth and Christianity."[44] Yates and Moulton, in their *History of the State of New York*, reported that a certain Indian tribe in Missouri was still "retaining some ceremonies of the Christian worship."[45]

Parallels between Christian and Indian customs were enumerated. Some compared the Indian's custom of placing the dead person's feet east and head west to Christian burial customs.[46] It was reported that the Indians had a belief in heaven and hell, an afterlife of punishments and rewards for deeds done on earth.[47] Hence the Indians allegedly believed in the immortality of the soul,[48] a devil which they described as a "great Evil Spirit,"[49] and one God,[50] the "Great Spirit,"[51] creator of all things, unchangeable and omnipotent.[52] Ethan Smith even claimed the Indians believed in the Christian trinity, basing his opinion on the discovery in one Indian mound of what he called a "triune vessel," a vase formed of three human faces said to represent Indian gods. But, argued Smith, the "triune vessel" could be better interpreted as a representation of "one Jehovah in three persons."[53]

The earliest Spanish explorers of Central and South America had also been looking for Christian parallels. Large stone crosses found in Central America, for example, were cited as evidence that Christianity had been preached in ancient America. Cortez reported seeing a cross ten feet high near a temple in Central America. The Indians, he reported, "could nevre know the original how that God of Crosse came amongst them. . . . There is no memorie of anye Preaching of the Gospell."[54] Although the natives had no memory of Christianity, the stone crosses, according to early writer Francesco Clavigero, proved to many that "the Gospel had been preached in America some centuries before the arrival of the Spaniards."[55] Antonio del Rio included in his 1822 book a plate showing a codex of a Mayan offering sacrifice to one of these large stone crosses.[56] Actually these so-called crosses are stylized or conventionalized "world trees," a central element of the religious worship of the Aztec and Maya, who believed that such trees were placed at the four cardinal points and another in the center.[57]

A belief that Christianity had existed in the New World led naturally to questions about how the gospel could have been preached to the ancient Americans. In 1792 Jeremy Belknap phrased the question this way:

"If the gospel was designed for an universal benefit to mankind, why was it not brought by the Apostles to America?" He continued, "To solve this difficulty it has been alleged that America was known to the ancients; and that it was enlightened by the personal ministry of the Apostles."[58]

Belknap's question implies that he doubted such a possibility, but many did not. Congregational clergyman Samuel Mather argued in 1773 that Christ had commissioned his apostles to go into all the world to preach the gospel (Matt. 28:19-20) and that the apostle Paul had declared that the gospel had been preached to every creature under heaven (Col. 1:23); therefore there were good reasons for believing that the gospel had been preached to the ancient Americans. Mather himself believed that the apostles and perhaps even some of the seventy disciples might have visited America and preached the gospel. Although the Indians of "this Western World sinned away the Gospel," Mather hoped that through his preaching they would one day be "restored" to the true Christian faith.[59]

Early Spanish explorers and priests also promoted the story that the apostles once came to America to preach the gospel. The Mexican god Quetzalcoatl, described as a man with white skin, was identified by some Spaniards as St. Thomas. Francesco Clavigero, who personally doubted the story of St. Thomas's visit to America, wrote:

> Dr. Siguenza imagined that the Quetzalcoatl, deified by these people [Mexicans], was no other than the apostle St. Thomas, who announced to them the Gospel. . . . Some Mexican writers are persuaded that the Gospel had been preached in America some centuries before the arrival of the Spaniards. The grounds of that opinion are some crosses which have been found at different times, which seem to have been made before the arrival of the Spaniards: the fast of forty days observed by the people of the new world, the tradition of the future arrival of a strange people, with beards, and the prints of human feet impressed upon some stones, which are supposed to be the footsteps of the apostle St. Thomas.[60]

The legend of St. Thomas's visit to America was repeated by Paul Cabrera and others.[61] But the legend of Quetzalcoatl had other interpretations.

At least one early writer, Chevalier Boturini (1702-51), found the legend of Quetzalcoatl more suggestive of Christ himself.[62] Ethan Smith was also fascinated by Quetzalcoatl—"the most mysterious being of the whole Mexican mythology"—but he was equivocal in his identification. Smith described him as "a white and bearded man" and as both a "high priest" and a "legislator." Smith thus united in one figure the tradition of Moses the lawgiver and of Aaron the high priest. Unlike Moses, however, Quetzalcoatl "preached peace to men, and would permit no other offerings to the Divinity than the first fruits of the harvests." Smith also compared the healing power of the "serpent of the green plumage," a symbol for Quetzalcoatl, with Moses' "brazen serpent in the wilderness."[63] The New Testament, of course, draws a parallel between the brazen serpent which was lifted up in the wilderness and the Son of God who was lifted on the cross (John 3:14). After preaching to the ancient Americans, this white god disappeared promising one day to return.[64] In reality the legend of the ancient god Quetzalcoatl was conflated by the Indians with the story of a tenth-century A.D. ruler named Topiltzin, who reportedly had fair skin and a beard. He had left his people under embarrassing circumstances, promising to return one day. Thus the bearded Cortez was met by the Aztec leader Montezuma as the returning god.[65]

Samuel Sewall, a commissioner of the Society for the Propagation of the Gospel in New England, pointed to another biblical passage which he thought helped to place the Indians in God's scheme of things. He, like Ethan Smith, based his imperative to preach the gospel to the Indians on a belief that they were in fact of Israelite descent. In a work he published in Boston in 1697, Sewall quoted the passage from John 10:16 in which Christ refers to other sheep of a different fold to whom the gospel will be preached. Sewall noted one Protestant theologian who interpreted the "other sheep" as a reference to the ten tribes. "If it be no haeresie to say, the Ten Tribes are the Sheep," argued Sewall, "Why should it be accounted Haeresie to say America is the distinct Fold there implied? For Christ doth not affirm that there shall be one Fold; but that there shall be ONE FLOCK, ONE SHEPHERD!"[66] Sewall believed that the passage prophesied that the Indians would hear Christ's "voice" when he would eventually come to America and establish the New Jerusalem.[67]

Early nineteenth-century Americans thus had available to them two seemingly contradictory traditions about the Indians and their ancestors. On the one hand, Indians were savages—at best lazy and slothful, at worst murderers and devil worshipers—entirely incapable of civilization. On the other, they were degenerate Jews who had every possibility of being restored to their former civilized condition. Those who cast the Indians as inherently "savage," however, had to explain the existence of the earthen works in North America as well as the great stone buildings and temples of Mexico and Peru.

Many could only reconcile such contradictions by proposing that there simply must have once been a civilized, productive group in America in addition to the Indians. Ethan Smith's optimistic assessment of Indian potential led him to propose that the Indians had separated from the more civilized tribes, resorted to hunting, and eventually degenerated into wild savages. In time, he speculated, the Indians destroyed their more peaceful brethren, somewhere in North America. This theme he repeated several times:

> Israel brought into this new continent a considerable degree of civilization; and the better part of them long laboured to maintain it. But others fell into the hunting and consequent savage state; whose barbarous hordes invaded their more civilized brethren, and eventually annihilated most of them, and all in these northern regions![68]

> But the savage tribes prevailed; and in time their savage jealousies and rage annihilated their more civilized brethren.[69]

> It is highly probable that the more civilized part of the tribes of Israel, after they settled in America, became wholly separated from the hunting and savage tribes of their brethren; that the latter lost the knowledge of their having descended from the same family with themselves; that the more civilized part continued for many centuries; that tremendous wars were frequent between them and their savage brethren, till the former became extinct. . . . No other hypothesis occurs to mind, which appears by any means so probable.[70]

Ethan Smith was not the only proponent of the possibility that there were two groups of people in ancient America. Indeed, he only adapted a theory which was already widely held in late eighteenth- and early nineteenth-century America. His unique adaptation reconciled his own belief about the origin of the Indians and his personal imperative for missionary work among them. His belief that the Indians were descendants of the lost ten tribes who came to a land "where never mankind dwelt" compelled him to construct a theory which posited two groups of Indians but only one migration from the Old World. Previous writers had posited one migration for mound builders and another for Indians. But even some who did not necessarily believe that the Indians were of Israelite descent found the theory about two groups compelling. Jeremy Belknap, speaking to the Massachusetts Historical Society in 1792, articulated the theory in this way:

> Mounds and fortifications of a regular construction were discovered in the thickest shades of the American forest, overgrown with trees of immense age, which are supposed to be not the first growth upon the spot since the dereliction of its ancient possessors.
> The most obvious mode of solving the difficulty which arose in the curious mind on this occasion was by making inquiry of the natives. But the structures are too ancient for their tradition. . . . Indeed the form and materials of these works seem to indicate the existence of a race of men in a stage of improvement superior to those natives of whom we or our fathers have had any knowledge; who had different ideas of convenience and utility; who were more patient of labour, and better acquainted with the art of defence.

> ... At what remote period these works were erected and by whom; what became of their builders; whether they were driven away or destroyed by a more fierce and savage people, the Goths and Vandals of America [Indians]; or whether they voluntarily migrated to a distant region; and where that region is, are questions which at present can not be satisfactorily answered.[71]

Governor DeWitt Clinton also believed in two groups. Interested in the Indian mounds of his state, he personally visited many of them and speculated about their origins at a meeting of the New York Historical Society in 1811:

> There is every reason to believe, that previous to the occupancy of this country by the progenitors of the present nations of Indians, it was inhabited by a race of men, much more populous, and much further advanced in civilization. The numerous remains of ancient fortifications, which are found in this country, ... demonstrates a population far exceeding that of the Indians when this country was first settled.[72]

Clinton speculated that in ancient times a large group from northern Asia migrated to North America. Once in America they built mighty cities and became numerous. In time, they were invaded and attacked by a more savage group from Asia and eventually annihilated. "And the fortifications," he concluded, "are the only remaining monuments of these ancient and exterminated nations."[73]

John Yates and Joseph Moulton related an Indian legend in their 1824 history of New York which seemed to corroborate such a theory: "Before and after that remote period, when the ancestors of the Senecas sprung into existence, the country, especially about the lakes, was thickly inhabited by a race of civil, enterprising, and industrious people, who were totally destroyed, and whose improvements were taken possession of by the Senecas."[74]

Solomon Spalding wove his story around the mound-builder myth. He described two distinct nations: the one lived in huts, hunted, and were uncivilized, dark-skinned savages; the other built houses and cities, worked metals, kept records, tilled the earth, domesticated animals, wore clothes like Europeans, and were a fair-skinned civilized people.[75]

Such sentiments found their way into newspaper accounts, even in the neighborhood where Joseph Smith grew up. In 1818 the *Palmyra Register* opined that the mound builders "had made much greater advances in the arts of civilized life" than any Indians, and the *Palmyra Herald* declared in 1823 that the fortifications were "the work of some other people than the Indians."[76]

These mound builders were believed by some to have been a white-skinned race. Ethan Smith referred to James Adair's remark that "the Indians have their tradition, that in the nation from which they originally came, all were of one colour."[77] The color, according to Smith, was "white," as the Indians "have brought down a tradition, that their former ancestors, away in a distant region from which they came, were white."[78] In 1816 the Philadelphia *Port Folio* reported that "it is a very general opinion, prevailing in the western country, that there is ample proof that the country in general was once inhabited by a civilized and agricultural people" who were eventually destroyed by the Indians.[79] "It is a current opinion," the periodical continued, "that the first inhabitants of the western country were white people."[80] One Indian tradition reportedly held "Kentucky had once been inhabited by white people, but that they were exterminated by the Indians."[81] Yates and Moulton also argued that the mounds and fortifications had been constructed by a white race which had been destroyed by the Indians in the Great Lakes region.[82]

Much debate centered on the Indian's skin color. Those most eager to promote the pre-Adamite theory emphasized the different skin colors among the nations as evidence of separate creations, but conservative Christians tried to explain the difference as a result of climatic and environmental influences and thus to keep the dark-skinned peoples in the family of Adam. One skirmish in this debate was initiated by Lord Kames (Henry Home) in his book *Sketches of the History of Man*. Kames rejected the climate theory, referring instead to the diversity of color as evidence of separate creations.[83] His ideas were subsequently attacked by the Reverend Samuel Stanhope Smith of Philadelphia and by James Adair. Both argued that the Indian's skin color was due to climatic and environmental conditions. Wrote Adair:

> Many incidents and observations lead me to believe, that the Indian colour is not natural; but that the external difference between them and the whites, proceeds entirely from their custom and method of living, and not from any inherent spring of nature. . . . That the Indian colour is merely accidental, or artificial, appears pretty evident.[84]

Adair believed that the reddish color was not the original one. In his travels he had seen Indians of various hues, he wrote, even white Indians. The Indians also had a tradition that they were once all of one color but they did not know which. However, according to Adair, they seemed to prefer dark skin since they would constantly anoint their bodies with bear grease mixed with a red root. He also observed that the years of exposing their bodies to "parching winds, and hot sun-beams" had tarnished their skin with a "tawny red colour." If the Indians' ancestors had also persisted in painting their skin and exposing their bodies to the sun, Adair speculated that nature might have effected a permanent change: "We may easily conclude then, what a fixt change of colour, such a constant method of life would produce: for the colour being once thoroughly established, nature would, as it were, forget herself, not to beget her own likeness."[85] Adair was encouraged in this belief by stories of strange births. He had it on "good authority," he wrote, that a negro child had been born to a Spanish woman "by means of a black picture that hung on the wall, opposite to the bed where she lay." He also heard of the birth of two white children to black parents and the birth of a white child to Indian parents long before the arrival of white men.[86] Adair therefore found it reasonable to assume that the Indians' ancestors, due to climatic and environmental conditions, gave birth to dark-skinned children.

Late in the nineteenth century, the director of the Smithsonian's Bureau of Ethnology, J. W. Powell, assessed the popularity of these beliefs which by that time had been superseded. "It is difficult to exaggerate the prevalence of this romantic fallacy, or the force with which the hypothetic 'lost races' had taken possession of the imaginations of men," he wrote. "For more than a century the ghosts of a vanished nation have ambuscaded in the vast solitudes of the continent, and the forest-covered mounds have been usually regarded as the mysterious sepulchers of its kings and nobles."[87]

The mound-builder myth thus made manageable for many Americans a complex of persistent problems with the Indians. Traditions persisted that the ancient inhabitants of the Americas had demonstrated knowledge of Jewish law and Christianity. Certainly the archaeological record displayed evidence of what white settlers would term "civilization"— cities, temples, and fortifications. Yet Americans had come to justify their harsh behavior towards the Indians—taking their land, proselytizing only half-heartedly—by talking about the Indians' inherent savagery, their inability to be civilized. The mound-builder myth reconciled such contradictory ideas about the Indians. Early Mormons quickly took advantage of the situation, reported the *Unitarian* in 1834, by claiming that the North American mounds were "proofs that this country was once inhabited by a race of people better acquainted with the arts of civilized life, than the present race of savages; and this, they contend, is satisfactory presumptive proof of the truth of the [Book of Mormon's] history."[88]

The Book of Mormon's explanation is that shortly after Lehi's family arrived in the New World, Lehi died and his colony divided into two major groups. The civilized, peaceful group, called Nephites after Lehi's righteous son Nephi, built cities, worked metals, kept records, tilled the earth, managed flocks, and wore clothing. The uncivilized group, called Lamanites after Lehi's oldest and rebellious son Laman, lived in tents, hunted, went virtually naked,[89] and were savage warriors. The savage group thus descended from the civilized one, just as in Ethan Smith's theory.[90]

The Nephites were a "white and delightsome" people, but the Lord eventually cursed the Lamanites with "a skin of blackness" for their wickedness (2 Ne. 5:21). Thus a people of Jewish descent became dark-complexioned. However, when the Lamanites repented of their sins "their curse was taken from them, and their skin became white like unto the Nephites" (3 Ne. 2:15). Moreover, the Book of Mormon promises that when the latter-day Indians repent, "many generations shall not pass away among them, save they shall be a white and delightsome people" (2 Ne. 30:6).[91] Thus the editor of the *Vermont Patriot and State Gazette*, a paper published in Montpelier, could acknowledge in an 1831 article that one object of the Book of Mormon was to give "the cause of the dark complexion of the native inhabitants of the forests."[92] Such an answer was significant for a generation who saw the various skin colors as a challenge to their belief that all men were descendants of one white-skinned man, Adam. The Book of Mormon is not explicit about how the metamorphosis from white to dark or dark to white takes place, but the Lamanites' curse came only after they had "dwindled in unbelief" (1 Ne. 12:23; Morm. 5:15). While a few instantly turned white (3 Ne. 2:15), the Book of Mormon explains that latter-day Indian converts will become white within a few generations (2 Ne. 30:6). Although there were stories circulating about a few eighteenth-century Indians turning white,[93] Joseph Smith evidently believed that the change in the Indian's skin color would result from a gradual and natural process. In 1831 he reportedly told missionaries that it was the Lord's will that they should take Indian women as their wives in order that the Lamanite "posterity may become white, delightsome and just."[94]

The Book of Mormon's description of the Lamanites sometimes sounds like an exaggerated version of contemporary stereotypes about North American Indians. After their separation from the Nephites, the Lamanites were led by their "evil nature" to become "wild, and ferocious, and a blood-thirsty people, full of idolatry and filthiness; feeding upon beasts of prey; dwelling in tents, and wandering about in the wilderness with a short skin girdle about their loins and their heads shaven; and their skill was in the bow, and in the cimeter, and the ax. And many of them did eat nothing save it was raw meat" (Enos 20). When dissident Nephites joined with the Lamanites, they "marked themselves with red in their foreheads after the manner of the Lamanites" (Al. 3:4). Moroni records that the Lamanites were cruel to their prisoners of war, raping and "torturing their bodies even unto death" (Moro. 9:9-10).

The Nephites were continually harassed by the Lamanites. Late in the fourth century A.D., the Nephites were driven by the Lamanites into "the land northward" where they were destroyed in a region described as having "large bodies of water" and "many waters, rivers, and fountains" (He. 3:4; Morm. 6:4), presumably referring to the Great Lakes region.

The Book of Mormon describes the Lamanites as practicing both idolatry and human sacrifice. They took many Nephite prisoners, writes the Nephite prophet Mormon, "both women and children, and did offer them up as sacrifices unto their idol gods" (Morm. 4:14, 21). And when the Lamanites are discovered by Europeans, they will still be a "dark, and loathsome, and a filthy people, full of idleness and all manner of abominations" (1 Ne. 12:23).

The Nephites, on the other hand, are described as "industrious" (2 Ne. 5:17, 24). They preserved a knowledge of the Hebrew and Egyptian languages (Morm. 9:32-34). Nephi explained that he made his record "in the language of my father, which consists of the learning of the Jews and the language of the Egyptians" (1 Ne. 1:2). Since the Book of Mormon claims to have been written in "reformed Egyptian" characters (Morm. 9:32), some scholars have concluded that Nephi meant that he wrote Hebrew words using Egyptian script.[95] This description seems similar to the early nineteenth-century habit of comparing the Indian's language to Hebrew and their pictographs to Egyptian hieroglyphics. The Nephites also kept the "law of Moses" (2 Ne. 25:24-30) and possessed "the five books of Moses" and other Old Testament scriptures (1 Ne. 5:10-22). The Book of Mormon actually gives few details of the observance of the law. It mentions temples but not the ceremonies, priests but not their robes or temple duties. The Nephites, according to the book, observed the Sabbath (Jar. 5) and offered sacrifices and burnt offerings from the "firstlings of their flocks" (Mos. 2:3).[96]

The Book of Mormon has been called "the American Gospel" because it contains an account of the visit of the resurrected Jesus Christ to America (3 Ne. 11-26). It describes Christ, in words reminiscent of some descriptions of Quetzalcoatl, as both a "high priest" (Al. 13) and "he that gave the law" (3 Ne. 15:5), who taught the Nephites that their posterity would assist one day in building the New Jerusalem in America (3 Ne. 20:15-22, 21:22-25; see also Eth. 13:1-12). He said that those in America were his "other sheep" and promised one day to return (3 Ne. 15:21-24). Thus the Book of Mormon solves the problem of how the gospel came to ancient America.

The Book of Mormon overtly discusses the ramifications of such ideas for early American history. It details, for example, a vision given to Nephi in which he foresees the early history of America. The vision portrays a sense of mission for America which parallels the self-proclaimed views of many Puritans and other Americans.[97] God inspires Columbus to discover "the promised land" of America (1 Ne. 13:10-12). Seeking religious freedom, the Puritans and Pilgrims are later led "out of captivity" to the New World, bringing with them the Bible which they preach to the Indians (1 Ne. 13:13-24, 38). "The wrath of God" is upon the Indians, and they are scattered and smitten by the early white settlers (1 Ne. 13:14). The Revolutionary War is won by the aid of God, and a nation under God is founded (1 Ne. 13:17-18, 30). The new nation is to be "a land of liberty" with no king as long as they obey God's commandments (2 Ne. 10:11). Again the Indians are scattered, this time by the Americans, but the Lord will not allow them to be completely destroyed (1 Ne. 13:30-32). Later the Book of Mormon returns to this topic of early American history and explains in terms which would have pleased proponents of *vacuum domicilium* why the colonists were successful against the Indians:

> But behold, when the time cometh that they [the Lamanites] shall dwindle in unbelief, . . . if the day shall come that they will reject the Holy One of Israel, the true Messiah, their Redeemer and their God, behold, the judgments of him that is just shall rest upon them. Yea, he will bring other nations unto them, and he will give unto them power, and he will take away from them the lands of their possessions, and he will cause them to be scattered and smitten. (2 Ne. 1:10-11)

Though the Book of Mormon is perhaps harsher than Ethan Smith in its judgment of the Indians, with such adjectives as wild, ferocious, bloodthirsty, filthy, idle, loathsome, abominable, and drunken, it shares his enthusiasm for Christianizing the Indians. "And for this very purpose are these plates preserved," Joseph Smith was told in a revelation in July 1828, "that the Lamanites [Indians] might come to the knowledge of their fathers, and that they might know the promises of the Lord, and that they may believe the gospel" (D&C 3:19-20; see also Enos 11-18). The title page of the Book of Mormon states that its purpose is to show the Indians "what great things the Lord hath done for their fathers; and that they may know the covenants of the Lord, that they are not cast off forever."

The mound builder myth embodied the values, ideals, aspirations, assumptions, prejudices, and fears of early nineteenth-century Americans. The mound builders were white, agriculturalist, industrious, and Christian. The myth also reinforced prejudice against the Indians and justified fear of Indian vengeance. Thus the mound-builder myth flourished despite contrary evidence. In 1803 the Reverend James Madison of Virginia published an essay questioning the lost-race theory

INDIANS AND MOUND BUILDERS

and reasoning that the Indians had built the earth works.[98] In 1805 Thomas Jefferson demonstrated that the mounds contained the remains of those who had been buried over a period of time rather than the single mass burial of those killed in battle.[99] Even earlier, explorers had discovered Indian tribes inhabiting palisaded towns.[100]

Near the end of the century, such observations finally began to undermine the popularity of the myth. By 1890 the Smithsonian's J. W. Powell could finally write:

> The spade and pick, in the hands of patient and sagacious investigators, have every year brought to light facts tending more and more strongly to prove that the mounds, defensive, mortuary and domiciliary, which have excited so much curiosity and become the subject of so many hypotheses, were constructed by the historic Indians of our land and their lineal ancestors.[101]

Archaeologists generally believe the mound-builder culture of eastern North America began around 1000 B.C., lasted until about A.D. 1700, and was generally divided into two groups, the Adena and the Hopewell. The Adena culture of Ohio and surrounding states dates from 1000 B.C. or earlier and represents the Woodland tradition which lasted until about A.D. 700. The Adena buried their dead in conical and animal-shaped mounds such as the Great Serpent Mound in Ohio, built about two thousand years ago. The demise of this culture is difficult to date, but the Adena apparently overlapped the Hopewell culture of the Mississippi tradition, which began sometime between A.D. 200 and 500 and is responsible for stockaded towns and temple mounds such as Monks Mound in Cahokia, Illinois. Although for uncertain reasons Hopewell culture began to decline around A.D. 1000, they continued to use burial mounds and to construct stockaded towns until about A.D. 1700.[102]

Conclusion

Confronted with the task of making a final assessment of this study, I am keenly aware of the controversial nature of the subject, especially as it pertains to the historicity of the Book of Mormon. Indeed, this question once sharply divided "believer" from "non-believer," but the division may no longer be quite as clear. For various reasons an increasing number of faithful Mormons are suggesting that it may be possible to question the Book of Mormon's historicity and yet maintain a belief in its sacred and inspired nature.[1] They have joined with non-Mormon scholars in a search for clues from Joseph Smith's environment which might help to better understand the origin of Mormonism and its founding scripture: the Book of Mormon.

The more traditional elements of the Mormon community have tended to reject the possibility of early nineteenth-century influences on the Book of Mormon. Some maintain, for example, that cultural parallels are weak, contrived, or insignificant.[2] Others claim that there were no sources at all from which Joseph Smith might have taken his ideas; in other words, for this group the Book of Mormon was unique in its time.[3] Those who hold to this latter view may be the most vulnerable to the cultural evidences discussed in this book. For such a position suffers from a limited knowledge of Joseph Smith's environment and the pre-1830 literature on the subject of Indian antiquity. I have attempted to show that the cultural and literary evidence is not only plentiful but striking.

Those who question the value of historical criticism have made unfortunate statements about the situation existing when Joseph Smith published the Book of Mormon in 1830. One Mormon writer, for example, claimed that Joseph's "description of the stone box containing the golden plates stood alone for nearly a century as the only account involving ancient stone boxes."[4] Others have asserted that "there were no records on metal plates known in the Western World."[5] During the famous 1884 Braden and Kelley debate, Elder E. L. Kelley of the Reorganized Church of Jesus Christ of Latter Day Saints expressed a claim many Mormons today would no doubt assent to when he said that "there was no understanding and no knowledge extant in the world of the grand civilization that had occupied [the American continent] . . .

prior to 1834."[6] And sixty years later Mormon writer Milton R. Hunter added that Joseph Smith could not have known about "white Indians."[7] As has become evident, however, these and similar statements are inaccurate. Both stone boxes and metal plates were found in the mounds prior to 1830. Knowledge of North, Central, and South American antiquities was wide spread before the publication of the Book of Mormon. And the idea that the mound builders were a white-skinned, Christian people was a common assumption in Joseph Smith's day.

The foregoing analysis, to be sure, will not satisfy the intellectual and religious demands of everyone, and debate will of necessity continue. Realistically, the most that can be hoped for is that this work will encourage others adhering to the new school of Mormon scholarship to continue their research into the cultural-environmental aspects of the Book of Mormon. Without this, I believe, the Book of Mormon will barely be understood by its modern readers.

I have tried in this study to follow relevant historical-critical methods to discover the origin of a particular idea and to trace its change and development. Only after this can thoughtful readers determine how a work of literature fits against its cultural background. That some of the major features of the Book of Mormon's history of ancient America originated centuries before in religiously motivated minds and subsequently proved inaccurate would seem to argue in favor of the book's modern origin. Those readers who continue to maintain the Book of Mormon's ancient historicity must do so in the face of what I consider to be some rather clear indications to the contrary.

I have traced the idea that the Indians came to the New World as migrant Jews from its sixteenth-century European origin to its modern demise. Even informed Mormon scholars have had to concede that the American Indians are predominately of Mongolian extraction and that their ancestors inhabited the Americas throughout Book of Mormon times.[8] The theological issues which produced and supported the ten tribe and other Jewish theories no longer trouble theologians. Although some in Joseph Smith's day correctly concluded that the Mongolians had crossed the Bering Strait, others clearly guessed wrong.

The same is true of the theory that a lost race built the mounds but were later destroyed by aboriginal Indians. Archaeologists now know that the Indians built the mounds and that mound-builder cultures still existed at the time of the European discovery of the New World. The theory originated in order to explain Indian inferiority and to justify the taking of Indian lands. The demise of this myth may be one of the most impressive challenges to the Book of Mormon's ancient origins.

CONCLUSION

Furthermore, I have tried to illuminate the Book of Mormon by attempting to recapture the intellectual milieu of Joseph Smith's day through an examination of the pre-1830 literature. But I have intentionally avoided making direct connections. As I. Woodbridge Riley wrote more than eighty years ago:

> How far did Joseph Smith fasten on this literary driftwood, as it floated on the current of the times? It is here unnecessary to follow the ebb and flow of the tide of speculation. In spite of a continuous stream of conjectural literature, it is as yet impossible to pick out any special document as an original source of the Book of Mormon.[9]

This study, I believe, has a much wider scope than simply trying to correct misconceptions regarding the Book of Mormon's origins and history: it encourages readers to obtain a more accurate view of the Book of Mormon itself and to form some idea of the emotional climate and cultural environment in which it emerged, to unify and expand the field of vision, and to make useful investigations instead of promulgating illusory and emotional speculations concerning the unknown. The better one understands the pre-1830 environment of Joseph Smith, the better he or she will understand the Book of Mormon. This, I conclude, is the challenge facing future Book of Mormon scholarship.

Endnotes

NOTES TO THE INTRODUCTION

1. Alexander Campbell, "The Mormonites," *Millennial Harbinger* 2 (Feb. 1831): 93.
2. Jason Whitman, "The Book of Mormon," *Unitarian* (Boston), 1 Jan. 1834, 47.
3. In 1834 E. D. Howe, using information from disaffected Mormon Philastus Hurlbut, claimed that the Book of Mormon was really a reworking of the Spalding manuscript. *Mormonism Unvailed* (Painesville, OH, 1834), 278-90. For a discussion of the origin and development of the Spalding theory, see Lester E. Bush, Jr., "The Spalding Theory Then and Now," *Dialogue: A Journal of Mormon Thought* 10 (Autumn 1977): 40-69.
4. Blanke's article is found in *Amerikastudien* 25 (1980), 3: 243-68; Mernitz's essay is in *The John Whitmer Historical Association Journal* 2 (1982): 30-37; and Thomas's article is in *Sunstone* 8 (May-June 1983): 19-25.
5. See the following discussions of the theory that Joseph Smith conceptually translated the Book of Mormon: B. H. Roberts, *Defense of the Faith and the Saints*, 2 vols. (Salt Lake City: Deseret News, 1907-12), 1:255-74; Richard Van Wagoner and Steven Walker, "Joseph Smith: 'The Gift of Seeing,'" *Dialogue: A Journal of Mormon Thought* 15 (Summer 1982): 49-68; Edward H. Ashment, "The Book of Mormon—A Literal Translation?" *Sunstone* 5 (March-April 1980): 10-14; James E. Lancaster, "The Method of Translation of the Book of Mormon," *The John Whitmer Historical Association Journal* 3 (1983): 51-61. This theory does not account for the early eye-witness accounts which describe the translation process as literal and mechanical. See Dan Vogel, "Is the Book of Mormon a Translation? A Response to Edward H. Ashment," *Journal of Pastoral Practice* 5 (1982), 3: 75-91.
6. Blake T. Ostler, "A Pseudepigraphic Theory of the Book of Mormon," forthcoming in *Dialogue: A Journal of Mormon Thought* 19 (Fall 1986), 3.
7. Among those who have recognized possible anti-masonic elements in the Book of Mormon are Fawn M. Brodie, *No Man Knows My History: The Life of Joseph Smith*, 2nd ed., rev. and enl. (New York: Alfred A. Knopf, 1976), 63-66; Thomas F. O'Dea, *The Mormons* (Chicago: University of Chicago Press, 1957), 35; Jerald and Sandra Tanner, *Mormonism: Shadow or Reality?*, enl. ed. (Salt Lake City: Modern Microfilm, 1982), 69-72; Robert N. Hullinger, *Mormon Answer to Skepticism, Why Joseph Smith Wrote the Book of Mormon* (St. Louis: Clayton Publishing House, 1980), 100-119;

H. Michael Marquardt, "Early Nineteenth Century Events Reflected in the Book of Mormon," *Journal of Pastoral Practice* 3 (1979), 1: 118-20; and Mernitz. Richard L. Bushman, *Joseph Smith and the Beginnings of Mormonism* (Urbana: University of Illinois Press, 1984), 128-31, provides an apologetic response. See also John E. Thompson, "Joseph Smith and the Illuminati: Masonry and Anti-Masonry in the Burned-over District," unpublished paper, 1980, much of which was incorporated in *The Masons, the Mormons, and the Morgan Incident* (Ames: Iowa Research Lodge No. 2, 1984).

8. Among those who have recognized possible anti-Catholic elements in the Book of Mormon are Brodie, 59-60; O'Dea, 34; and Mernitz, 33-34.

9. Only a few writers have discussed possible anti-Universalist elements in the Book of Mormon. See Thomas, "Revival Language," and his "Lehi's Plan of Salvation Discourse in Its Nineteenth Century Theological Setting," unpublished paper, 1984.

10. Marjorie Nicolson and Nora Mohler, "The Scientific Background of the Voyage to Laputa," *Annals of Science* (1937), as discussed in S. H. Gould, "Gulliver and the Moons of Mars," *Journal of the History of Ideas* 6 (Jan. 1945): 91-101.

11. Ibid., 95-96.

12. On the theological significance of America's discovery, see Lewis Hanke, "The Theological Significance of the Discovery of America," in Fredi Chiappelli, ed., *First Images of America: The Impact of the New World on the Old*, 2 vols. (Berkeley and Los Angeles: University of Califoirnia Press, 1976), 1:363-89; and Blanke.

13. *Times and Seasons*, 1 March 1842, 707-708; cf. Joseph Smith, Jr., *History of the Church of Jesus Christ of Latter-day Saints*, B. H. Roberts, ed., 6 vols. (Salt Lake City: Deseret Book Co., 1932-51), 4:537-38. Smith's letter to Wentworth, especially the portion quoted, appears to have been adapted from Orson Pratt's pamphlet, *A[n] Interesting Account of Several Remarkable Visions and of the Late Discovery of Ancient American Records* (Edinburgh, 1840).

14. Robert F. Berkhofer, Jr., *The White Man's Indian: Images of the American Indian from Columbus to the Present* (New York: Alfred A. Knopf, 1978), 3. Berkhofer discusses in detail the process by which the Europeans "invented" the Indians and wielded the concept to their own advantage.

15. Samuel Williams, *The Natural and Civil History of Vermont* (Walpole, NH, 1794), 187. See also Ethan Smith, *View of the Hebrews; or the Tribes of Israel in America* (Poultney, VT, 1825), 88, which quotes Samuel Williams and others describing the Indians as a unitary group.

16. For a discussion of Ethan Smith's possible influence on the Book of Mormon as well as a review of the polemics of that theory, see Hullinger, 172-76. See also George D. Smith, "Book of Mormon Difficulties," *Sunstone* 6 (May-June 1981): 45-50; Madison U. Sowell, "The Comparative Method Reexamined," *Sunstone* 6 (May-June 1981): 44, 50-54; and David Persuitte, *Joseph Smith and the Origins of the Book of Mormon* (Jefferson, NC: McFarland and Co., 1985). Persuitte's book contains valuable material on Ethan Smith but overstates his influence and enters into unnecessary and tenuous speculations.

17. Horatio Gates Spafford, *A Gazetteer of the State of New York* (Albany, 1824), 400-401.

NOTES TO CHAPTER ONE 77

18. For information on Palmyra in the 1820s, consult Milton V. Backman, Jr., *Joseph Smith's First Vision: Confirming Evidences and Contemporary Accounts*, 2nd ed., rev. and enl. (Salt Lake City: Bookcraft, 1980), 22-52.

19. B. H. Roberts, *Studies of the Book of Mormon*, Brigham D. Madsen, ed. (Urbana: University of Illinois Press, 1985), 153-54. Others who have discussed the Roberts manuscripts include Wesley P. Walters, "The Origin of the Book of Mormon," *Journal of Pastoral Practice* 3 (1979), 3: 123-52; and George D. Smith, " 'Is There Any Way to Escape These Difficulties?': The Book of Mormon Studies of B. H. Roberts," *Dialogue: A Journal of Mormon Thought* 17 (Summer 1984): 94-111.

20. Joseph Smith's Puritan ancestry and Solomon Mack's exploits with the Indians are discussed in Richard Lloyd Anderson, *Joseph Smith's New England Heritage: Influence of Grandfathers Solomon Mack and Asael Smith* (Salt Lake City: Deseret Book Co., 1971).

NOTES TO CHAPTER 1

1. Parley P. Pratt, Jr., ed., *The Autobiography of Parley P. Pratt* (Salt Lake City: Deseret Book Co., 1938), 54-56.

2. Lucy [Mack] Smith, *Biographical Sketches of Joseph Smith the Prophet, and His Progenitors for Many Generations* (Liverpool, England, 1853), 152.

3. Ibid., 91-92.

4. Joseph Smith to Josiah Stowell, 18 June 1825, in *Church News*, 12 May 1985, 10. The letter is discussed in Marvin S. Hill, "Richard L. Bushman—Scholar and Apologist," *Journal of Mormon History* 11 (1984): 130-33; and in *Time*, 20 May 1985, 44. See note 17.

5. "Articles of Agreement" [dated 1 November 1825], *Daily [Salt Lake City] Tribune*, 23 April 1880, in Francis W. Kirkham, *A New Witness for Christ in America: The Book of Mormon*, 2 vols., enl. ed. (Salt Lake City: Utah Printing Co., 1947-59), 1:492-94.

6. "Answers to Questions," *Elders' Journal*, 1 (July 1838): 43; cf. Joseph Smith, Jr., *History of the Church of Jesus Christ of Latter-day Saints*, B. H. Roberts, ed., 6 vols. (Salt Lake City: Deseret Book Co., 1932-51), 3:29.

7. Emily M. Austin, for example, testified that Joseph Smith told the money diggers to sacrifice a dog (Emily M. Austin, *Mormonism; or, Life Among the Mormons* [Madison, WI, 1882], 32-33). This incident was apparently discussed at Smith's 1830 trial in Colesville; Judge Joel K. Noble remembered testimony to that effect. See Wesley P. Walters, "From Occult to Cult with Joseph Smith, Jr.," *Journal of Pastoral Practice* 1 (1977), 2: 125, 135. Another example of the Smith family's use of magic devices is given by neighbor William Stafford who described Joseph Smith, Sr., drawing a magic circle and placing stakes around the supposed treasure (E. D. Howe, *Mormonism Unvailed* [Painesville, OH, 1834], 238-39). See Andrew Barton [Thomas Forrest], *The Disappointment; or, the Force of Credulity*, David Mays, ed. (Gainesville: University Press of Florida, 1976), esp. 89, for a satire on money digging originally published in New York in 1767 which contains an interesting

parallel to the placing of stakes in a circle around the treasure. On the reliability of Stafford's and others' testimony regarding Joseph Smith's early magic and money-digging practices, see Rodger I. Anderson, "Joseph Smith's Early Reputation Revisited," *Journal of Pastoral Practice* 4 (1980), 3: 71-108, and 4 (1980), 4: 72-105.

8. The preliminary draft of her history is located in Mormon church archives, Salt Lake City, and is quoted in Walters, "From Occult to Cult," 127. On the blend of folk magic and popular religion, see Jon Butler, "Magic, Astrology, and the Early American Religious Heritage, 1600-1760," *American Historical Review* 84 (April 1979): 317-46. See also Keith Thomas, *Religion and the Decline of Magic* (New York: Scribners, 1971), for a general treatment of folk magic and its suppression by the religiously orthodox.

9. Charles Marshall, "The Original Prophet," *Fraser's Magazine* 7 (Feb. 1873): 229. A discussion of the documentation on the 1826 trial can be found in Wesley P. Walters, "Joseph Smith's Bainbridge, N.Y., Court Trials," *Westminster Theological Journal* 36 (Winter 1974): 123-55.

10. See Walters, "From Occult to Cult," 125.

11. "Mormonism—No. II," *Tiffany's Monthly* 5 (1859): 164-65.

12. Ibid., 165.

13. Dean Jessee, ed., "Joseph Knight's Recollection of Early Mormon History," *Brigham Young University Studies* 17 (Autumn 1976): 32-33; Smith, *Biographical Sketches*, 99.

14. Although Smith would later use "angel" when referring to the personage, many of the early sources use "spirit": e.g., Howe, 242, 275-76; *The [Rochester] Gem*, 5 Sept. 1829; and Martin Harris to W. W. Phelps, 23 Oct. 1830 (see note 17). Smith, in the *History of the Church* 1:14, and in an earlier version of the story in Dean C. Jessee, ed., *The Personal Writings of Joseph Smith* (Salt Lake City: Deseret Book Co., 1984), 7, reported that the messenger appeared three times.

15. Several sources report that Smith used his stone to find the plates: e.g., *Tiffany's Monthly* 5 (1859): 163, 169; Howe, 252; and Harris to Phelps, 23 Oct. 1830.

16. Howe, 242.

17. Harris to Phelps, 23 Oct. 1830, in *Church News*, 28 April 1985, 6. The letter is discussed in Hill, 130-33, and in *Time*, 20 May 1985, 44. I am aware of the recent controversy surrounding this letter, as well as the Joseph Smith, Jr., to Josiah Stowell letter (see note 4). It is beyond the scope of this analysis to deal with either of these documents at great length. The particulars they reveal can be found in other contemporary sources. See, for example, John Phillip Walker, ed., *Dale Morgan on Early Mormonism: Correspondence and a New History* (Salt Lake City: Signature Books, 1986), 219-319. Consequently, while they are important to the early years of Joseph Smith and, I believe, are valuable documents that deserve critical scrutiny, they are not essential to my approach to the Book of Mormon.

18. *Latter Day Saints' Messenger and Advocate* 2 (Oct. 1835): 197-98. Smith's collaboration with Cowdery is announced in 1 (Oct. 1834): 13.

19. Smith, *History of the Church*, 1: 16.

20. Jessee, *Writings of Joseph Smith*, 7; Smith, *Biographical Sketches*, 85-86; Jessee, "Joseph Knight's Recollection," 31.
21. Smith, *Biographical Sketches*, 85.
22. *Tiffany's Monthly* 5 (1859): 167; cf. Jessee, "Joseph Knight's Recollection," 33-34.
23. *Tiffany's Monthly* 5 (1859): 169.
24. Smith, *Biographical Sketches*, 109.
25. The *Gem*, 5 Sept. 1829; *Advertiser and Telegraph* (Rochester), 31 Aug. 1829. Both sources are quoted in full in Kirkham, 2:31-32. The use of "spectacles" in the early part of the translation and the use of a "seer stone" in the latter part is discussed in James E. Lancaster, " 'By the Gift and Power of God,' " RLDS *Saints' Herald*, 15 Nov. 1962, 15-17; and Richard Van Wagoner and Steven Walker, "Joseph Smith: 'The Gift of Seeing,' " *Dialogue: A Journal of Mormon Thought* 15 (Summer 1982): 53-54.
26. David Whitmer, *An Address to All Believers in Christ* (Richmond, MO, 1887), 12.
27. *Wayne Sentinel* (Palmyra), 16 Feb. 1825. For a survey of early American folklore about money digging, consult Wayland D. Hand, "The Quest for Buried Treasure: A Chapter in American Folk Legendry," in Nikolai Burlakoff and Carl Lindahl, eds., *Folklore on Two Continents: Essays in Honor of Linda Degh* (Bloomington, IN: Trickster Press, 1980), 112-19; Gerard T. Hurley, "Buried Treasure Tales in America," *Western Folklore* 10 (July 1951): 191-216.
28. *Wayne Sentinel* (Palmyra), 27 Dec. 1825.
29. James Hall, *Legends of the West* (Philadelphia, 1832), 59. In the preface Hall claims: "The legends now presented to the public are entirely fictitious; but they are founded upon incidents which have been witnessed by the author during a long residence in the Western States, or upon traditions preserved by the people, and have received but little artificial embellishment."
30. Sarah Josepha Hale, *Traits of American Life* (Philadelphia, 1835), 100-110. Although writing a work of fiction, Hale insists that the story, places, and names are true. Her verse narrative *The Genius of Oblivion* (Concord, NH, 1823) describes fugitives from Tyre who sail to ancient America.
31. That the Indians buried treasures with their dead is reported in James Adair, *The History of the American Indians* (London, 1775), 178; Thaddeus Mason Harris, *The Journal of a Tour into the Territory Northwest of the Alleghany Mountains; Made in the Spring of the Year 1803* (Boston, 1805), 165.
32. James Axtell, *The European and the Indian: Essays in the Ethnohistory of Colonial North America* (New York: Oxford University Press, 1981), 117-20; Dwight B. Heath, ed., *A Journal of the Pilgrims at Plymouth: Mourt's Relation* (New York: Corinth Books, 1963), 21, 27-28, 34. This book was originally published in London in 1622.
33. E[phraim] G. Squier, *Antiquities of the State of New York* (Buffalo, 1851), 97.
34. Smith, *History of the Church*, 2:79.
35. Ibid., 3:37.
36. Jessee, *Writings of Joseph Smith*, 358.

37. *Fraser's Magazine* 7 (Feb. 1873): 229-30.
38. *Historical Magazine* 7 (May 1870): 307.
39. *Tiffany's Monthly* 5 (1859): 164.
40. Caleb Atwater, "Descriptions of the Antiquities Discovered in the State of Ohio and Other Western States," *Archaeologia Americana: Transactions and Collections of the American Antiquarian Society* 1 (1820): 162. Other contemporary accounts of stone boxes can be found in John Haywood, *The Natural and Aboriginal History of Tennessee* (Nashville, 1823), 196, 199-203, 348; *Nashville Whig*, 12 Dec. 1818, 5 July 1820.
41. Haywood, 196.
42. Squier, 224; J. W. Powell, ed., *Twelfth Annual Report of the Bureau of Ethnology, 1890-1891* (Washington, D.C.: Government Printing Office, 1894), 334-36, 351-53, 690-701; David I. Bushnell, Jr., *Native Cemeteries and Forms of Burial East of the Mississippi*, Smithsonian Institution Bureau of American Ethnology, Bulletin 71 (Washington, D.C.: Government Printing Office, 1920), 44-58; William A. Ritchie, *The Archaeology of New York State* (Garden City, NY: Natural History Press, 1965), 214.
43. Adair, 179.
44. Harris, 153. Harris's unusual mention of copper breastplates—copper was thought too soft for armor—finds an interesting parallel in the Book of Mormon (see Mos. 8:10).
45. O[rsamus] Turner, *Pioneer History of the Holland Purchase of Western New York* (Buffalo, 1850), 668-69.
46. "Of the Aborigines of the Western Country," pt. 2, *Port Folio* (Philadelphia), fourth series, 2 (July 1816): 1.
47. Haywood, 82. Joseph Smith may have combined these stories of plates coming from the mounds with detailed descriptions of metal books used by the Jews and others in the Old World. In 1842 he described the plates as "bound together . . . with three rings" (*History of the Church*, 4:537). The Apocrypha mentions that the Jews wrote on "tables of brass" (1 Mac. 8:22, 14:18-19). Johann Jahn wrote in 1823 that "those [ancient] books, which were inscribed on tablets of wood, lead, brass, or ivory, were connected together by rings at the back, through which a rod was passed to carry them by" (*Jahn's Biblical Archaeology*, Thomas C. Upham, trans. [Andover, 1823], 95-96). Cf. *The Evening and the Morning Star* 1 (Jan. 1833), in which W. W. Phelps quotes from Jahn's book. Thomas Hartwell Horne, *An Introduction to the Study of Bibliography*, 2 vols. (London, 1814), 1:33-35, discusses the ancient use of lead books and brass and copper plates; Claudius Buchanan, *The Star in the East*, 10th Amer. ed. (Boston, 1811), 48-49, says that the Jews of Cochin, India, who Buchanan believed were remnants of the lost ten tribes, kept a history of their journey to those parts on "plates of brass"; Bernard de Montfaucon, *Antiquity Explained, and Represented in Sculptures*, 2 vols. (London, 1721), 2:241-42, contains a description and drawing of an Egyptian gnostic book of lead. See also H. Curtis Wright, "Metallic Documents of Antiquity," *Brigham Young University Studies* 10 (Summer 1970): 469, who points out that curses and black magic are usually found on lead or tin whereas beneficial texts are

inscribed on gold or silver. In this context Jesse Smith's 17 June 1829 letter to Hyrum Smith that "the story is that the gold book proved to be lead" takes on added significance (Joseph Smith Letter Books, Mormon church archives).

48. J. W. Powell, ed., *Fifth Annual Report of the Bureau of Ethnology, 1883-1884* (Washington, D.C.: Government Printing Office, 1887), 98-107.

49. Ethan Smith, *View of the Hebrews; or the Tribes of Israel in America*, 2nd ed. (Poultney, VT, 1825), 130, 217-25; Elias Boudinot, *A Star in the West; or a Humble Attempt to Discover the Long Lost Ten Tribes of Israel* (Trenton, 1816), 110-11; Charles Beatty, *The Journal of a Two Months Tour* (London, 1768), 90; Israel Worsley, *A View of the American Indians* (London, 1828), 116, 182.

50. Smith, *View of the Hebrews*, 223. The first edition of Smith's book appeared in 1823, but its popularity required a second 1825 edition. The first edition was reviewed in various contemporary periodicals, excerpts of which, were included in the second edition. A lengthy selection of Smith's book was included in Josiah Priest's *The Wonders of Nature and Providence, Displayed* (Albany, 1825), 297-332 (Manchester Library, accession number 208). Israel Worsley relied heavily on Smith's work, and many other writers used Smith's book as an authoritative source. Moreover, one review from the *Christian Advocate* (Saratoga, NY) and two letters from New York—one from the Reverend Hyde of Eden, the other from the Reverend Proudfit of Salem—preface the second edition. The book was also reviewed in the Utica *Christian Repository*, May 1825, and Priest published his book in Albany. These and other references indicate that Ethan Smith's book was widely read and known in the New York area.

51. Smith, *View of the Hebrews*, 130.

52. Solomon Spalding, *The "Manuscript Found." Manuscript Story, by Rev. Solomon Spaulding, Deceased* (Liverpool: Millennial Star Office, 1910), 1-2. Spalding's manuscript was published by the Reorganized Church of Jesus Christ of Latter Day Saints in 1885, and by the Church of Jesus Christ of Latter-day Saints in 1886, 1903, 1908, and 1910. The mound on the Conneaut River referred to by Spalding is possibly the same one described in Atwater, 124. For an interesting parallel to Spalding's imaginary discovery, see the account of a stone-lined vault containing a skeleton and some engraved brass rings which Irishman Thomas Ashe discovered under a large stone at the summit of a mound of earth (*Travels in America* [London, 1808], 1:308-18).

NOTES TO CHAPTER 2

1. Manasseh ben Israel, *The Hope of Israel*, Moses Wall, trans. (London, 1652), 22.

2. Ibid., 21-22.

3. Thomas Thorowgood and John Eliot, *Jews in America, or Probabilities, that those Indians are Judaical, made more probable by some Additionals to the former Conjectures* (London, 1660). 35. According to Antonoine Simon

82 NOTES TO CHAPTER TWO

le Page Du Pratz, author of *The History of Louisiana* (London, 1774), the Indians of Louisiana built their temples on mounds and constructed them like the Jews with two compartments. See the *Columbian Magazine* (Philadelphia) 2 (May 1788): 240.

4. [William Moulton], *A Concise Extract, from the Sea Journal of William Moulton* (Utica, NY, 1804), 122.

5. Elijah Parish, *A New System of Modern Geography* (Newburyport, MA, 1810), 138. On the use of Parish's *Geography* in schools, see Allen Johnson, ed., "Elijah Parish," *Dictionary of American Bibliography*, 22 vols. (New York: Charles Scribner's Sons, 1928-58), 14:204.

6. Alexander [von] Humboldt, *Political Essay on the Kingdom of New Spain*, trans. John Black, 4 vols. (London, 1811), 2:69-70. See p. 63 for the Teotihuacan pyramids, pp. 193-95 for Cholula and other Central American pyramids, and p. 64 for speculations about the ages of the structures.

7. Ethan Smith, *View of the Hebrews; or the Tribes of Israel in America* (Poultney, VT, 1825), 177, 179.

8. Antonio del Rio, *Description of the Ruins of an Ancient City, Discovered Near Palenque, in the Kingdom of Guatemala* (London, 1822).

9. John V[an] N[ess] Yates and Joseph W[hite] Moulton, *History of the State of New York* (New York, 1824), 73-77.

10. Mark Beaufoy, *Mexican Illustrations* (London, 1828), 218-23; W[illiam] Bullock, *Six Months Residence and Travels in Mexico* (London, 1824), 331; Domingo Juarros, *A Statistical and Commercial History of the Kingdom of Guatemala*, J[ohn] Baily, trans. (London, 1823), 18-19; John Ranking, *Remarks on the Ruins at Palenque, in Guatemala, and on the Origin of the American Indians* (London, 1828).

11. Beaufoy, 189-91, 218.

12. Bullock, 330.

13. Juarros, 171-72, 187, 383.

14. John Haywood, *The Natural and Aboriginal History of Tennessee* (Nashville, 1823), 77, 94-95.

15. "Aborigines of America" pt. 1, *American Monthly Magazine* (Boston) 1 (April 1829): 41-46.

16. Thaddeus Mason Harris, *The Journal of a Tour into the Territory Northwest of the Alleghany Mountains; Made in the Spring of the Year 1803* (Boston, 1805), 147-48.

17. Smith, *View of the Hebrews*, 199.

18. Quoted in ibid., 199.

19. *Palmyra Herald*, 19 Feb. 1823.

20. Smith, *View of the Hebrews*, 189, 200-201.

21. Jedidiah Morse, *The History of America*, 2 vols. (Philadelphia, 1808), 1:98.

22. H. M. Brackenridge to Thomas Jefferson, 25 July 1813, in *The Belles-Lettres Repository* (New York) 1 (1 Aug. 1819): 291. Cf. *Niles' Weekly Register* (Baltimore) 16, supplement (1819): 89.

23. DeWitt Clinton, "A Memoir on the Antiquities of the Western parts of the State of New-York," *Transactions of the Literary and Philosophical Society of New York* 2 (1815-25): 82.

NOTES TO CHAPTER TWO

24. Caleb Atwater, "Description of the Antiquities Discovered in the State of Ohio and Other Western States," *Archaeologia Americana: Transactions and Collections of the American Antiquarian Society* 1 (1820): 179. Atwater's statement about Ohio being a "vast cemetery" is quoted in Yates and Moulton, 20. In a letter addressed to the postmaster of Nauvoo, Illinois, dated 16 November 1842, Atwater stated that his work had "a very extensive circulation" and suggested that the Mormons reprint it as a companion volume to the Book of Mormon (copy in Stanley Ivins Collection, Utah State Historical Society, Salt Lake City).

25. Harris, 159.

26. "Indian Antiquities," *Palmyra Register*, 21 Jan. 1818. Cf. *North American Review* 16 (Nov. 1817): 137.

27. Atwater, 132. See his description of stone fortifications, 131-33, 145-51.

28. Ibid., 126-27.

29. Ibid., 151, 145.

30. Harris, 157.

31. Solomon Spalding, *The "Manuscript Found." Manuscript Story, by Rev. Solomon Spaulding, Deceased* (Liverpool: Millennial Star Office, 1910), 54.

32. DeWitt Clinton, *Discourse Delivered before the New-York Historical Society* (New York, 1812), 53-54.

33. Yates and Moulton, 13-14.

34. Fawn M. Brodie, *No Man Knows My History: The Life of Joseph Smith*, 2nd ed., rev. and enl. (New York: Alfred A. Knopf, 1976), 19.

35. Cyrus Thomas, *Catalogue of Prehistoric Works East of the Rocky Mountains*, Smithsonian Institution Bureau of Ethnology, Bulletin No. 12 (Washington, D.C.: Government Printing Office, 1891), 148.

36. Ibid., 149; E[phraim] G. Squier, *Antiquities of the State of New York* (Buffalo: George H. Derby and Co., 1851), 89-90.

37. Thomas, 148; Squier, 55. DeWitt Clinton visited the mounds at Canandaigua in 1811 and described them in his *Discourse*, 53-54. For more about the Smith family business in Canandaigua, see Lucy [Mack] Smith, *Biographical Sketches of Joseph Smith the Prophet, and His Progenitors for Many Generations* (Liverpool, 1853), 92, 95-96, 98; Lucy Smith to Mary Pierce, 23 Jan. 1829, in the *Ensign*, Oct. 1982, 70-73; Joseph Smith to Josiah Stowell, 18 June 1825, in the *Church News*, 12 May 1985.

38. For various sources, some strong and some weak, which trace Smith's pre-1830 movements in such towns as Macedon, Geneva, Seneca Falls, and South Bainbridge, see Larry C. Porter, "A Study of the Origins of the Church of Jesus Christ of Latter-day Saints in the States of New York and Pennsylvania, 1816-1831," Ph.D. diss., Brigham Young University, 1971, 65, 77, 80.

39. Thomas, 148; Squier, 85-86.

40. Thomas, 140; Squier, 46-47.

41. Thomas, 140; Squier, 46. Thomas also lists "twenty-five distinct embankments, adjacent to each other, about 4 miles south of Oxford" (140).

42. Clinton, "Memoir on Antiquities," 2:81.

43. Courtesy of Wesley P. Walters. For further information on the Oxford mound, see Thomas F. Gordon, *Gazetteer of the State of New York* (Philadelphia, 1836), 392; Henry Galpin, *Annals of Oxford* (Oxford, NY: Times Book and Job Printing House, 1906), 51-53.

44. Thomas, 150; Squier, 15. On the location of Smith's relatives, see Richard Lloyd Anderson, *Joseph Smith's New England Heritage: Influences of Grandfathers Solomon Mack and Asael Smith* (Salt Lake City: Deseret Book Co., 1971), 213, 215.

45. James Sullivan, *The History of the District of Main* (Boston, 1795), 83.

46. Harris, 165-66.

47. Yates and Moulton, 19.

48. *Columbian Historian*, 20 Aug. 1824, 69.

49. "Aborigines of America," pt. 2, *American Monthly Magazine* 1 (May 1829): 80-81. Caleb Atwater discussed the controvery in his letter to the Nauvoo postmaster, 16 November 1842:

> Great doubts exist as to . . . whether they came from Asia across at Behring's straits, and journeying onwards to Western New York; Then, progressing slowly in a south western direction until they reached Mexico and Peru: or, starting from the last countries, they moved in a north eastern direction to Western New York. Perhaps, your prophet has found the records which they left buried in the earth, which inform us of all the migrations of that ancient people.

50. John Kilbourn, *The Ohio Gazetteer*, 6th ed. (Columbus, 1819), 20.

51. Harris, 153.

52. Clinton, *Discourse*, 60.

53. Smith, *View of the Hebrews*, 193.

54. Ibid., 194-95.

55. "Antiquities of the West," *Port Folio* (Philadelphia), fourth series, 7 (April 1819): 350.

56. Haywood, 348-49, 111.

57. Atwater, 232, 176. Cf. *Columbian Historian*, 3 Sept. 1824, 86; Haywood, 349.

58. Harris, 153, 166.

59. Smith, *View of the Hebrews*, 172, 192-98.

60. On the North American Indians' knowledge of metallurgy, see, among others, Dudley T. Easby, Jr., "Early Metallurgy in the New World," *Scientific American* 214 (April 1966): 73-81; and Harold E. Driver, *Indians of North America* (Chicago: University of Chicago Press, 1961), 175-78.

61. This is discussed in Robert Silverberg, *Mound Builders of Ancient America: The Archaeology of a Myth* (Greenwich, CT: New York Graphic Society, 1968), 67-68.

62. Harris, 154-55.

63. Patrick Gass, *A Journal of the Voyage and Travels of a Corpse of Discovery* (Pittsburgh, 1807), 35.

64. Smith, *View of the Hebrews*, 198.

65. Clinton, *Discourse*, 58.

NOTES TO CHAPTER TWO

66. William A. Ritchie, *The Archaeology of New York State* (Garden City, NY: Natural History Press, 1965), 274, 286; William A. Ritchie, *A Prehistoric Fortified Village Site at Candandaigua, Ontario County, New York*, Research Records of the Rochester Museum of Arts and Sciences, no. 3 (Rochester, 1936).

67. *Brattleboro Messenger* (Brattleboro, VT), 30 Oct. 1830.

68. The traditional view of Book of Mormon geography was consistently held by Joseph Smith and the early church until the first decade of the twentieth century when B. H. Roberts questioned it for apologetic reasons. M. T. Lamb's 1887 book, *The Golden Bible; or, the Book of Mormon. Is it from God?* (New York: Ward and Drummond) had outlined problems regarding long-distance travel and rapid population growth in the Book of Mormon, and Roberts believed that such problems could only be solved by postulating a limited geographic area for Book of Mormon events. See his *New Witness for God*, 3 vols. (Salt Lake City: Deseret News, 1909), 3:503. However, Roberts was aware of traditional and exegetical problems with a limited geography for the Book of Mormon. See *Studies of the Book of Mormon*, Brigham D. Madsen, ed. (Urbana: University of Illinois Press, 1985), 92-93, 252-53. From Roberts's day until the present, Mormon writers have persistently sought to find a smaller geographic area in which to place Book of Mormon events.

Brigham Young University anthropologist John L. Sorenson's 1985 book, *An Ancient American Setting for the Book of Mormon* (Salt Lake City: Deseret Book and the Foundation for Ancient Research and Mormon Studies), is the most ambitious work yet to appear. However, Sorenson's attempt to limit Book of Mormon events to Mesoamerica—the region immediately surrounding the Isthmus of Tehuantepec in southern Mexico—has serious problems, in my opinion. First, Sorenson has been unable to overcome Mormon traditions regarding Book of Mormon events outside his limited area. Second, he has unnecessarily distorted Book of Mormon passages which do not fit his theory (e.g., Al. 22:32). Third, he has excused, minimized, or ignored contradictory evidence. I have dealt with Sorenson's theory in detail in "A Preliminary Examination of the New Theory of Book of Mormon Geography," unpublished paper, 1985.

69. Franklin D. Richards and James A. Little, *A Compendium of the Doctrines of the Gospel*, 2nd ed. (Salt Lake City, 1884), 289; *Times and Seasons*, 15 Sept. 1842, 922. Sorenson's doubts regarding Joseph Smith's authorship of "Lehi's Travels" (1-2) are without foundation.

70. For Joseph Smith calling North America the "land of desolation," see Levi Ward Hancock, *The Life of Levi W. Hancock*, typewritten copy, Brigham Young University Library, in John H. Wittorf, "Joseph Smith and the Prehistoric Mound Builders of Eastern North America," *Newsletter and Proceedings of the Society for Early Historic Archaeology*, No. 123 (Oct. 1970): 8; W. W. Phelps also referred to the North American prairies as the "land desolation" in *The Evening and the Morning Star*, Oct. 1832; *Latter Day Saints' Messenger and Advocate*, July 1836, 341.

71. *Times and Seasons*, 15 Dec. 1844, 746-47.

72. Caleb Atwater, "On the Prairies and Barrens of the West," *American Journal of Science* 1 (1818): 120-24.

73. Edmund Burke's description is typical: "[The New World] is composed of two vast continents, one on the North, the other upon the South, which are joined by the great kingdom of Mexico, which forms a sort of isthmus fifteen hundred miles long, and in one part, at Darien, so extremely narrow, as to make the communication between the two oceans by no means difficult" (*An Account of the European Settlements in America*, 2 vols, 2nd ed. [London, 1758], 1:204). In 1842 the editor of the *Times and Seasons* reflected this same view: "They [the Nephites] lived about the narrow neck of land, which now embraces Central America, with all the cities that can be found" (3:915). And Mormon leader Parley P. Pratt compared the ruins which John L. Stephens discovered in Central America to cities built on the Book of Mormon's neck of land (*Millennial Star*, March 1842, 165).

74. Joseph Smith to Emma Smith, 4 June 1834, in Dean C. Jessee, ed., *The Personal Writings of Joseph Smith* (Salt Lake City: Deseret Book Co., 1984), 324. The letter was written the day after Smith had made an inspired declaration that a skeleton the men had unearthed from an Indian burial mound was that of "Zelph'—'a white Lamanite" and "a warrior under the great prophet Onaneagus that was known from the hill Camorah [sic] or east sea to the Rocky mountains" (Scott G. Kenney, ed., *Wilford Woodruff's Journal*, 9 vols. [Midvale, Utah: Signature Books, 1983-85], 1:10).

75. In 1835 Oliver Cowdery described the hill in western New York from which Joseph Smith had taken the plates: "At about one mile west rises another ridge of less height, running parallel with the former . . . between these hills, the entire power and national strength of both the Jaredites and Nephites were destroyed. . . . He [Mormon] deposited . . . all the records in this same hill, Cumorah" (*Latter Day Saints' Messenger and Advocate*, July 1835, 158). It is important to note that Cowdery claims the help of Smith in preparing his account (1:13).

76. *Contributor* (Salt Lake City) 11 (May 1890): 265.

77. [David Marks], *The Life of David Marks* (Limerick, ME, [1831]), 341.

78. Jason Whitman, "The Book of Mormon," *Unitarian* (Boston), 1 Jan. 1834, 43.

79. E[dward] S[trut] Abdy, *Journal of a Residence and Tour in the United States of North America, from April, 1833, to October, 1834*, 3 vols. (London, 1835), 3:57-58.

80. Charles [Blancher] Thompson, *Evidence in Proof of the Book of Mormon* (Batavia, NY, 1841), 101. See also *Times and Seasons*, 1 Jan. 1842, 640-44, for a positive review of Thompson's book.

NOTES TO CHAPTER 3

1. "The Book of Mormon," *The Evening and the Morning Star*, Jan. 1833.

2. P[arley]. P. Pratt, *A Voice of Warning* (New York, 1837), 135.

3. Jedidiah Morse, *The American Universal Geography*, 2 vols. (Boston, 1793), 1:75. Morse's book went through several editions before 1830 and was listed for sale at Pomeroy Tucker's bookstore in Palmyra under books "for

NOTES TO CHAPTER THREE

school." See the *Wayne Sentinel*, 5 May through 7 July 1824. The book is also listed in the Manchester Library under accession numbers 42 and 43.

4. *Explicatio totius astronomiae, Opera* (Geneva, 1658), 2:655, in Don Cameron Allen, *The Legend of Noah: Renaissance Rationalism in Art, Science, and Letters* (Urbana: University of Illinois Press, 1963), 133. For a general history of the pre-Adamite theory, see A. J. Maas, "Preadamites," *The Catholic Encyclopedia*, 15 vols. (New York: Gilmary Society, 1907-12), 12:370-71; O. W. Garrigan, *New Catholic Encyclopedia*, 17 vols. (New York: McGraw-Hill Book Co., 1967), 11:702; also Margaret T. Hodgen, *Early Anthropology in the Sixteenth and Seventeenth Centuries* (Philadelphia: University of Pennsylvania Press, 1964), 272-6; and Allen, 132-37.

5. Ronald B. McKerrow, ed., *The Works of Thomas Nashe*, 4 vols. (Oxford: Basil Blackwell, 1958), 2:116; see also 1:172.

6. This little-known conflict is discussed in Frederick S. Boas, ed., *The Works of Thomas Kyd* (Oxford: Clarendon Press, 1901), lxxi.

7. Quoted in McKerrow, 4:236.

8. The two works were first published in Latin in 1655. *Men before Adam* went through four editions in 1655, *Theological System* went through three. In 1656 both works were translated into English and bound together in one volume, though one is dated 1655 and the other 1656.

9. Quoted in Allen, 133.

10. For a list of books issued in response to La Peyrere's pre-Adamite thesis, see Allen, 136-37. La Peyrere's influence on the French and English deists is discussed in David Rice McKee, "Isaac de la Peyrere, a Precursor of Eighteenth-Century Critical Deists," *Publications of the Modern Language Association of America* 59 (June 1944): 456-85.

11. Bernard Romans, *A Concise Natural History of East and West Florida*, 2 vols. (New York, 1775), 1:38.

12. Henry Home [Lord Kames], *Sketches on the History of Man*, 2 vols. (Edinburgh, 1774), 2:71.

13. Samuel Stanhope Smith, *An Essay on the Causes of the Variety of Complexion and Figure in the Human Species, To which are Added Strictures on Lord Kaims's Discourse, on the Original Diversity of Mankind* (Philadelphia, 1787), 22.

14. Romans, 38.

15. Francesco Saverio Clavigero, *The History of Mexico*, Charles Cullen, trans., 3 vols. (Philadelphia, 1817), 3:93-102. Clavigero's work was first translated into English in 1787 in London and went through several American editions before 1830. Several American authors also made use of Clavigero's work; for example, Josiah Priest quoted from Clavigero in *The Wonders of Nature and Providence, Displayed* (Albany, 1825), 569-93. Priest's book was listed in the Manchester Library under accession number 208. See note 43 for more information on Priest.

16. J. Eric S. Thompson, *The Rise and Fall of Maya Civilization* (Norman: University of Oklahoma Press, 1954), 261. For a discussion of the weakness of Indian flood stories as evidence for transcontinental diffusion, see Robert Wauchope, *Lost Tribes and Sunken Continents: Myth and Method in the Study of American Indians* (Chicago: University of Chicago Press, 1962), 64.

17. Antonio del Rio, *Description of the Ruins of an Ancient City, Discovered Near Palenque, in the Kingdom of Guatemala . . . Followed by Teatro Critico Americano; or, Critical Investigation and Research into the History of the Americans, by Doctor Paul Felix Cabrera* (London, 1822), 31.

18. The two manuscripts remained together in the Spanish archives until 1822 when London publisher Henry Berthoud had them translated into English and printed in a single volume. See publisher's preface: "Prefactory Address," vii-xiii.

19. This statement prefaces Rio's book on an unnumbered page.

20. Rio, 28-29.

21. Cotton Mather, *India Christiana. A Discourse, Delivered unto the Commissioners, for the Propagation of the Gospel among the American Indians* (Boston, 1721), 23.

22. Morse, 75.

23. Timothy Dwight, *Travels; in New-England and New-York*, 4 vols. (New Haven, 1821-22), 1:126.

24. The Carthaginian theory is discussed in Lee Eldridge Huddleston, *Origins of the American Indians: European Concepts, 1492-1729*, Latin American Monographs, no. 11 (Austin: University of Texas Press, 1967), 16-21.

25. For a discussion and bibliography on the Welsh-Indian theory, see Edward George Hartmann, *Americans from Wales* (Boston: Christopher Publishing House, 1976), 13-24, 228-29.

26. See Huddleston, 72-73, 92-94; also Lewis Hanke, *Aristotle and the American Indians: A Study in Race Prejudice in the Modern World* (Bloomington: Indiana University Press, 1975), 3.

27. Huddleston, 25.

28. Hamon L'Estrange, *Americans no Jewes, or Improbabilities that the Americans are of that race* (London, 1652). This book was probably published in 1651, though the date reads 1652.

29. Huddleston, 40-45, 57, 86-88. As early as 1671 John Ogilby mentioned the Jewish theories: "Some would derive the Americans from the Jews; others, from the ten Tribes of Israel, carry'd into captivity. The ground of which Opinions is, That the Jews and Israelites were scatter'd amongst all Nations; therefore they conclude, that America was also Peopled by them." John Ogilby, *America: Being the Latest, and Most Accurate Description of the New World* (London, 1671), 27.

30. Most eighteenth- and nineteenth-century scholars believed that the ten tribes had been scattered throughout Asia and the Middle East. See, for example, William Jones, *A Discourse on the Institution of a Society for Enquiring into the History . . . Antiquities, Arts, Sciences, and Literature of Asia* (London, 1784); Claudius Buchanan, *The Star in the East* (Boston, 1811) and *Christian Researches in Asia* (Boston, 1811). This view was also accepted by biblical commentator Adam Clarke who rejected the theory that the American Indians had descended from the ten tribes. *The Holy Bible . . . with a Commentary and Critical Notes*, 7 vols. (n.p., 1810), 2:535-36.

NOTES TO CHAPTER THREE

31. Huddleston, 34-35. The most comprehensive survey of the lost ten tribe literature is William Hart Blumenthal's "The Lost Ten Tribes," an enormous unpublished manuscript found in the American Jewish Archives, Cincinnati. A small section of the manuscript was published as *In Old America* (New York, 1930).

32. Manasseh ben Israel, *The Hope of Israel*, Moses Wall, trans. (London, 1652), 10-17. Manasseh ben Israel was first to publish Montenzinos's story in the 1650 Latin edition of his book.

33. The interpretation that Montezinos had seen Jews rather than Indians is in George Weiner, "America's Jewish Braves," *Mankind* 4 (Oct. 1974), 9:64. Jewish immigration to South America is covered in Jacob R. Marcus, *The Colonial American Jew, 1492-1776*, 3 vols. (Detroit: Wayne State University Press, 1970), 1:42-46; Cecil Roth, *A History of the Marranos*, 4th ed. (New York: Schocken Books, 1974), 271-95. The impact of the Mexican Inquisition on the Jews is discussed in Richard E. Greenleaf, *The Mexican Inquisition of the Sixteenth Century* (Albuquerque: University of New Mexico Press, 1969), 107-15, 162-71, 201-202, and *Zumarrage and the Mexican Inquisition*, 1536-43, Academy of American Franciscan History Monograph Series, vol. 4 (Richmond, VA: William Byrd Press, 1962), 89-99.

34. On the restoration of Israel and Judah, see, for example: Isa. 11:11-12; Jer. 3:12-18, 12:14-15, 30:3, 33:7-11; Ezek. 37. The idea that the restoration precedes the Messiah's coming is mostly implied from the context of such passages as Isa. 49-66; Ezek. 37-48; Joel 3; and Zech. 12-14.

35. On the scattering and restoration of Israel, see, for example: Deut. 28:64, 30:1-5; Isa. 11:11-12; Ezek. 36:24, 37:21. On the history of the Jews in England and Manasseh ben Israel's attempt to get them readmitted, see Cecil Roth, *A History of the Jews in England*, 3rd ed. (Oxford: Clarendon Press, 1964); Lucien Wolf, *Menasseh ben Israel's Mission to Oliver Cromwell* (London, 1901).

36. Tho[mas] Thorowgood, *Jews in America, or, Probabilities That the Americans are of that Race* (London, 1650). This work was apparently reprinted in 1652 (see Sabin, 95650, in the bibliography). Thomas Thorowgood and John Eliot, *Jews in America, or Probabilities that those Indians are Judaical, made more probable by some Addisionals to the former Conjectures* (London, 1660). This work seems to have been reprinted the same year (see Sabin, 95653).

37. Samuel Sewall, *Phaenomena Quaedam Apocalytica* (Boston, 1697), 1-2; Jonathan Edwards, *Observations on the Language of the Mahhekaneew Indians; in which . . . Some Instances of Analogy Between That and the Hebrew are Pointed Out* (New Haven, 1788).

38. [William Penn], *A Letter from William Penn* (London, 1683), 7; Roger Williams, *A Key into the Language of America* (London, 1643).

39. James Adair, *The History of the American Indians* (London, 1775), 3, 11.

40. See Wauchope, 57. Adair's distortions were generally recognized by contemporary scholars. See, for example, Samuel Farmer Jarvis, *Discourse on the Religion of the Indian Tribes of North America* [20 Dec. 1819] (New York, 1820), 10; C[onstantin] F[rancois] Volney, *View of the Climate and Soil of the United States of America* (London, 1804), 403.

41. Elias Boudinot, *A Star in the West; or, a Humble Attempt to Discover the Long Lost Tribes of Israel* (Trenton, 1816). The assertion that Boudinot visited Palmyra in 1820 during the fourth anniversary meeting of the American Bible Society is an error based on a misreading of an article in the *Palmyra Register*, 7 June 1820. The *Register* had reprinted an article from the *New York Column* and the reference to the meeting held in the hotel "in this city" means the New York City hotel. The error originated in Robert N. Hullinger's *Mormon Answer to Skepticism, Why Joseph Smith Wrote the Book of Mormon* (St. Louis: Clayton Publishing House, 1980), 33. Richard L. Bushman, *Joseph Smith and the Beginnings of Mormonism* (Urbana: University of Illinois Press, 1984), 234, follows Hullinger's error.

42. Fawn M. Brodie, *No Man Knows My History: The Life of Joseph Smith*, 2nd ed., rev. and enl. (New York: Alfred A. Knopf, 1976), 46.

43. Priest, *Wonders of Nature*, 297-332, contains a lengthy selection from Ethan Smith's work. Priest was a prominent peddler of chapbooks—cheap popular pamphlets of twenty-four pages or less; see James Truslow Adams, ed., *Dictionary of American History*, 7 vols. (New York: Charles Scribner's Sons, 1976), 1:494. Priest's *Wonders of Nature* as well as his *American Antiquities and Discoveries in the West* (Albany, 1833) contain extracts from many works and easily could have been compiled from previous chapbooks.

44. John V[an] N[ess] Yates and Joseph W[hite] Moulton, *History of the State of New York* (New York, 1824). The Yates-Moulton circular was published in the *Wayne Sentinel*, 28 April 1824; the publication announcement appears in the *Wayne Sentinel* for 20 April 1825.

45. Noah's speech was published in two issues of the *Wayne Sentinel*, 4 Oct. and 11 Oct. 1825. Noah's remark on the Israelite origin of the Indians comes from the later issue. The Ararat address was widely printed in New York newspapers and finally published under the title *Discourse on the Evidences of the American Indians Being Descendants of the Lost Tribes of Israel* (New York, 1837). A 22 October 1825 letter Noah wrote from New York indicates that he was influenced by the Indian-Israelite theories of Manasseh ben Israel, James Adair, and Elias Boudinot. See I. Herold Sharfman, *Jews on the Frontier* (Chicago: Henry Regnery Co., 1977), 214.

46. *Susquehanna Register* (Montrose, PA), 18 Jan. 1826.

47. Priest, *American Antiquities*, 73.

48. L'Estrange; see note 28.

49. *Utica Christian Repository* 4 (May 1825): 149.

50. Ethan Smith, *View of the Hebrews; or the Tribes of Israel in America* (Poultney, VT, 1825), 75.

51. [Samuel Mather], *An Attempt to Shew, that America Must be Known to the Ancients* (Boston, 1773), 13. Mather's books was known and discussed in New York as late as 1814. See *The New-York Magazine, and General Repository of Useful Knowledge* 1 (July 1814): 154-56.

52. Mather, *America Must be Known*, 18-19.

53. *Palmyra Herald*, 19 Feb. 1823.

54. Morse, 81.

55. Smith, 78.

NOTES TO CHAPTER THREE 91

56. James H[aines] McCulloh, Jr., *Researches on America: Being an Attempt to Settle Some Points Relative to the Aborigines of America, &c.* (Baltimore, 1817), 22-24.

57. See the *Columbian Historian* (New Richmond, OH), 17 June 1824, 9, which suggests that the animals were brought through the arctic zone by divine agency. Domingo Juarros believed the impossibility of migration of tropical animals through the arctic region forced one to accept a transoceanic crossing, probably shortly after the tower of Babel episode. Domingo Juarros, *A Statistical and Commercial History of the Kingdom of Guatemala*, J[ohn] Baily, trans. (London, 1823), 208-209.

58. P[ierre] [Francois Xavier] de Charlevoix, *Journal of a Voyage to North-America*, 2 vols (London, 1761), 1:1-59.

59. Ibid., 53. See also J[onathan] Carver, *Three Years Travels through the Interior Parts of North-America* (Philadelphia, 1796), 125-26.

60. *Palmyra Herald*, 19 Feb. 1823.

61. Carver, 117; William Robertson, *The History of America*, 2 vols. (London, 1777), 1:4.

62. [Antonoine Simon] le Page du Pratz, *The History of Louisiana* (London, 1774), 283.

63. McCulloh, 16.

64. Pratz, 283.

65. "Aborigines of America," pt. 2, *American Monthly Magazine* 1 (May 1829): 80-81.

66. Allen, 130-32.

67. Abraham Rees, *The Cyclopaedia; or, Universal Dictionary of Arts, Sciences, and Literature*, 41 vols. (Philadelphia, [1805-25]), states that neither the horse nor the ox were in America before the Spanish (see under "America," vol. 1, no pagination, alphabetically arranged); James Bentley Gordon, *An Historical and Geographical Memoir of the North-American Continent* (Dublin, 1820), 35-36, names the horse, the ox, the ass, the cow, the sheep, and the hog as Spanish imports; Lewis C[aleb] Beck, *A Gazetteer of the State of Illinois and Missouri* (Albany, 1823), 41, mentions the erroneous belief that the horse is indigenous to America.

68. Solomon Spalding, *The "Manuscript Found." Manuscript Story, by Rev. Solomon Spaulding, Deceased* (Liverpool: Millennial Star Office, 1910), 89.

69. Th[omas] Ashe, *Memoirs of Mammoth, Various Other Extraordinary and Stupendous Bones, of Incognita, or Non-Descript Animals, Found in the Vicinity of the Ohio, Wabash, Illinois, Mississippi, Missouri, Osage, and Read Rivers, &c. &c* (Liverpool, 1806).

70. *United States Literary Gazette* (Boston) 1 (1 June 1824): 77; *American Journal of Science and Arts* (New Haven) 14 (1828): 31-33.

71. Rembrandt Peale, *Account of the Skeleton of the Mammoth* (London, 1802) and *An Historical Disquisition on the Mammoth* (London, 1803).

72. *Port Folio* (Philadelphia), new series, 4 (7 Nov. 1807): 295-96. Both Peale's museum and the mammoth skeleton are discussed in Charles Coleman Sellers, *Charles Willson Peale*, 2 vols. (Philadelphia: American Philosophical Society, 1947), 2:137-44.

73. Samuel Williams, *The Natural and Civil History of Vermont* (Walpole, NH, 1794), 103.

74. Thomas Jefferson, *Notes on the State of Virginia* (Boston, 1802), 56; Manchester Library accession number 9.

75. George E. Lankford, "Pleistocene Animals in Folk Memory," *Journal of American Folklore* 93 (July-Sept. 1980): 293-304; Loren C. Eiseily, "Myth and Mammoth in Archaeology," *American Antiquity* 10 (Oct. 1945): 84-87.

76. *Royal American Magazine, or Universal Repository of Instruction and Amusement* (Boston), Sept. 1774, 350.

77. *Palmyra Herald*, 19 Feb. 1823.

78. Spalding, 18.

79. John Ranking, *Historical Researches on the Conquest of Peru, Mexico, Bogota, Natchez, and Talomeco, in the Thirteenth Century, by the Mongols, Accompanied with Elephants; and the Local Agreement of History and Tradition, with the Remains of Elephants and Mastodontes, Found in the New World* (London, 1827). 80.

80. Jeremy Belknap, *A Discourse, Intended to Commemorate the Discovery of America* (Boston, 1792), 43-44.

81. Yates and Moulton, 22.

82. Quoted in Lynn Glaser, *Indians or Jews?* (Gilroy, CA: Roy V. Boswell, 1973), 46.

83. Cotton Mather, *Magnalia Christi Americana; or, the Ecclesiastical History of New-England*, 2 vols. (Hartford, 1820), 1:15.

84. *Wayne Sentinel*, 24 July 1829.

85. Ibid.

86. *United States Literary Gazette*, 1 Jan. 1825, 294.

87. Smith, *View of the Hebrews*, 217.

88. Ibid., 130, 217-25. See Lee M. Friedman, "The Phylacteries Found at Pittsfield, Mass.," *Publications of the American Jewish Historical Society*, No. 25 (1917): 81-85, which gives evidence for the presence of Jews in the area. See also Sharfman, 210-11.

89. Elias Boudinot, 110-11; Charles Beatty, *The Journal of a Two Months' Tour* (London, 1768), 90; Israel Worsley, *A View of the American Indians* (London, 1828), 116, 182.

90. *United States Literary Gazette*, 1 Oct. 1824, 181; cf. Smith, *View of the Hebrews*, 280, in which the review is quoted.

91. *Vermont Patriot and State Gazette* (Montpelier), 19 Sept. 1831.

92. English theologian Sir Hamon L'Estrange also believed that those migrating from Babel "suffered no interruption by that confusion" (9).

93. The similarity between Ether's phrase "where there never had man been" and that of 2 Esdras 13:41, "where never mankind dwelt," was noted by B. H. Roberts, who also observed parallels between Jaredite and ten tribe migrations: both migrations are religiously motivated; both groups enter valleys at the commencement of their journeys; both travel north between the Tigris and Euphrates Rivers; both cross water barriers (the Jaredites crossed "many waters" and "the sea in the wilderness" before reaching the ocean, 2:6-7, 13; cf. 2 Esd. 13:40, 43-44); both trips take years; and both groups travel to

NOTES TO CHAPTER THREE 93

uninhabited lands. Paralleling Ethan Smith's interpretation that the uninhabited land mentioned in Esdras is America, Roberts interpreted Eth. 2:5 as a reference to the Jaredites' ultimate destination in the New World. See B. H. Roberts, *Studies of the Book of Mormon*, Brigham D. Madsen, ed. (Urbana: University of Illinois Press, 1985), 183-87. Brigham Young University religion professor Hugh Nibley also points out that the Jaredites crossed water barriers before reaching the ocean but prefers to interpret the uninhabited land of Eth. 2:5 as a reference to Asia rather than the New World. Hugh Nibley, *Lehi in the Desert and the World of the Jaredites* (Salt Lake City: Bookcraft, 1952), 175-78. Eth. 2:5 may therefore be saying that the Jaredites on their way to the New World passed through the same region that the ten tribes would later settle. Note the subtle difference between "where there never had man been" and "where never mankind dwelt."

94. W. W. Phelps saw the Book of Mormon's mention of "deseret" as an answer to the debate over the origin of the honey bee in the New World. *The Evening and the Morning Star*, July 1833. For those debating the origin of the honey bee in America, see, for example, Belknap, 117-24, and Jefferson, 102-103.

95. According to M. T. Lamb, the Book of Mormon's account of the Jaredite migration by sea has several problems: a 344-day sea voyage seems too long for such a journey, especially in light of the "furious wind" of Eth. 6:5; that all eight vessels remain and land together is difficult; and it would have been an insurmountable problem to divide people and animals between eight tiny vessels and to provide them all with food and fresh water to last nearly a year. *The Golden Bible; or, The Book of Mormon. Is It from God?* (New York: Ward and Drummond, 1887), 79-82.

96. On 1 May 1843, the *Times and Seasons* reported the discovery of some metal plates and a skeleton in a mound near Kinderhook, Illinois. The Mormons believed that a record of the Jaredites had been found and announced that it was "additional testimony to the authenticity of the Book of Mormon." Although the plates were fakes, Joseph Smith, according to William Clayton, "translated a portion and says they contain the history of the person with whom they were found, and he was a descendant of Ham through the loins of Pharoah, king of Egypt." Parley P. Pratt said the plates "are small and filled with engravings in Egyptian language and contain the genealogy of one of the ancient Jaredites back to Ham the son of Noah." For a discussion of the Kinderhook plates, together with the statements of Smith and Pratt, see Stanley B. Kimball, "Kinderhook Plates Brought to Joseph Smith Appear to Be a Nineteenth-Century Hoax," *Ensign*, Aug. 1981, 66-74; see also George D. Smith, "Joseph Smith and the Book of Mormon," *Free Inquiry* (Winter 1983): 23-24.

97. For a treatment of the evidence for the Mongolian origin of the American Indian, see, among others, Paul S. Martin, et al., *Indians Before Columbus; Twenty Thousand Years of North American History Revealed by Archaeology* (Chicago: University of Chicago Press, 1947); Diamond Jenness, ed., *The American Aborigines, Their Origin and Antiquity; a Collection of Papers by Ten Authors* (New York: Russell and Russell, 1972); and D'Arcy McNickle, *They Came Here First; the Epic of the American Indian* (Philadelphia: Lippincott, 1949).

NOTES TO CHAPTER 4

1. See J. H. Kennedy, *Jesuit and Savage in New France* (New Haven: Yale University Press, 1950).

2. The Puritan's initial optimistic estimation of the Indian's character is discussed in Alden T. Vaughan, *New England Frontier: Puritans and Indians, 1620-1675* (Boston: Little, Brown and Co., 1965), 43-46; and Gustav H. Blanke, "Early Theories About the Nature and Origin of the Indians, and the Advent of Mormonism," *Amerikastudien* 25 (1980), 3: 245-46.

3. Cotton Mather, *Magnalia Christi Americana; or, the Ecclesiastical History of New-England.*, 2 vols. (Hartford, 1820), 1:504.

4. Ibid., 503.

5. Cotton Mather, *India Christiana. A Discourse, Delivered unto the Commissioners, for the Propagation of the Gospel among the American Indians* (Boston, 1721), 28.

6. R[oger] Williams, *The Bloody Tenet Yet More Bloody* (London, 1652), 25. In another work, Williams summarized the Indian's religion: "The wandering Generations of Adams lost posterite, having lost the true and living God, their Maker, have created out of the Nothing of their owne inventions many false and fained Gods and Creators" (Roger Williams, *A Key into the Language of America* [London, 1643], 118).

7. For a discussion of Puritan and colonial reaction to Indian idolatry and human sacrifice, see Bernard W. Sheehan, *Savagism and Civility: Indians and Englishmen in Colonial Virginia* (Cambridge: Cambridge University Press, 1980), 44-46; Francis Jennings, *The Invasion of America: Indians, Colonialism, and the Cant of Conquest* (New York: W. W. Norton and Co., 1975), 46-47.

8. James Adair, *The History of the American Indians* (London, 1775), 199-200.

9. Quoted in Josiah Priest, *The Wonders of Nature and Providence, Displayed* (Albany, 1825), 575.

10. W[illiam] Bullock, *Six Months' Residence and Travels in Mexico* (London, 1824), 338; Alexander [von] Humboldt, *Political Essay on the Kingdom of New Spain*, John Black, trans., 4 vols. (London, 1811), 2:62.

11. On Indian alcoholism during the colonial and early American period, see Vaughan, 45-46; Brian W. Dippie, *The Vanishing American: White Attitudes and U.S. Indian Policy* (Middletown, CT: Wesleyan University Press, 1982), 34-36. The Indians' weakness for alcoholic beverages was noted by several early writers: Ethan Smith, *View of the Hebrews; or the Tribes of Israel in America* (Poultney, VT, 1825), 109-110; [Edmund Burke], *An Account of the European Settlements in America*, 2 vols. 2nd ed. (London, 1758), 1:169; and W. D. Cooper, *The History of North America* (New Brunswick, 1802), 2.

12. Quoted in James Buchanan, *Sketches of the History, Manners, and Customs, of the North American Indians, with A Plan for Their Melioration*, 2 vols. (New York, 1824), 1:19.

13. *Niles' Weekly Register* (Baltimore), 14 Nov. 1818, 185.

14. "An Account of the Vices peculiar to the Savages of N[orth] America," *Columbian Magazine, or Monthly Miscellany* (Philadelphia) 1 (Sept. 1786): 9.

NOTES TO CHAPTER FOUR

15. Puritan reaction to Indian idleness is discussed in Charles M. Segal and David C. Stineback, *Puritans, Indians, and Manifest Destiny* (New York: G. P. Putnam's Sons, 1977), 31-32, 46-47; Roy Harvey Pearce, "The 'Ruins of Mankind': The Indian and the Puritan Mind," *Journal of the History of Ideas* 13 (1952): 200-17; and Vaughan, 45.

16. Burke, 1:169; see also Cooper, 3; and Daniel Gookin, *Historical Collections of the Indians in New England* (Boston, 1792), 9.

17. The concept of *vacuum domicilium* was expressed as early as 1622 in *Mourt's Relation*. Under the heading "Reasons and Considerations touching the lawfulness of removing out of England into the parts of America," this source surveyed the actions of the biblical patriarchs and declared that it was "lawful now to take a land which none useth, and make use of it." See Dwight B. Heath, ed., *A Journal of the Pilgrims at Plymouth: Mourt's Relation* (New York: Corinth Books, 1963), 92.

18. John Cotton, *God's Promise to His Plantations* (Boston, 1634), 4-5.

19. Edmund Burke's statement that "their only occupations are hunting and war" became a typical characterization of the Indians both in Europe and America (1:169).

20. Roy Harvey Pearce, *The Savages of America: A study of the Indian and the Idea of Civilization*, rev. ed. (Baltimore: John Hopkins Press, 1965), 55.

21. See David Bidney, "The Idea of the Savage in North American Ethnohistory," *Journal of the History of Ideas* 15 (April 1954): 325; Dippie, passim.

22. Pearce, 61-62.

23. *Wayne Sentinel*, 11 Oct. 1825.

24. Smith, *View of the Hebrews*, 173-74.

25. Ibid., 175-76.

26. Ibid., 176-77.

27. Ibid., 248.

28. Ibid.

29. Ibid., 249.

30. Quoted in Robert Wauchope, *Lost Tribes and Sunken Continents: Myth and Method in the Study of American Indians* (Chicago: University of Chicago Press, 1962), 57.

31. Samuel Farmer Jarvis, *Discourse on the Religion of the Indian Tribes of North America* (New York, 1820), 8, 10.

32. Humboldt, *Political Essay*, 1:164-67. The willingness of missionaries to distort in order to convert is discussed in Charles S. Braden, *Religious Aspects of the Conquest of Mexico* (Durham, NC: Duke University Press, 1930), esp. 62-75; and Ursula Lamb, "Religious Conflicts in the Conquest of Mexico," *Journal of the History of Ideas* 17 (Oct. 1956): 526-39.

33. See, for example, Smith, *View of the Hebrews*, 156, 166-67; Charles Beatty, *The Journal of a Two Months' Tour* (London, 1768), 27, 84-92; Henry Ker, *Travels through the Western Interior of the United States, from the Year 1808 up to the Year 1816* (Elizabethtown, NJ, 1816), 151.

34. Smith, *View of the Hebrews*, 186, 220; Beatty, 90. Cf. 1 Ne. 5:10-22.

35. Smith, *View of the Hebrews*, 144; Ker, 152. Cf. 1 Ne. 5:11.

36. Ker, 152; cf. 1 Ne. 5:11; 2 Ne. 2.

37. Smith, *View of the Hebrews*, 120; Elias Boudinot, *A Star in the West; or, a Humble Attempt to Discover the Long Lost Ten Tribes of Israel* (Trenton, 1816), 114; Israel Worsley, *A View of the American Indians* (London, 1828), 117. Cf. He. 6:27.

38. Smith, *View of the Hebrews*, 115-16, 159; Boudinot, 112, 250; Worsley, 85, 117, 183; Beatty, 90; Ker, 152. Cf. Al. 10:22.

39. Smith, *View of the Hebrews*, 116; Boudinot, 113-14; Worsley, 117; Beatty, 90; Ker, 152. Cf. Eth. 1:3, 33.

40. Adair, 47-59.

41. [William Penn], *A Letter from William Penn* (London, 1683), 5.

42. Adair, 37-74; Boudinot, 89-107; Smith, *View of the Hebrews*, 89-95.

43. See, among others, Smith, *View of the Hebrews*, 182-85; Humboldt, *Political Essay*, 1:133-34, 140, 2:61; Humboldt, *Personal Narrative of Travels to the Equinoctial Regions of the New Continent, During the Years 1799-1804*, trans. Helen Maria Williams, 7 vols. (London, 1818-29), 6:323, 325; Bullock, 326; John V[an] N[ess] Yates and Joseph W[hite] Moulton, *History of the State of New York* (New York, 1824), 14-15; Antonio del Rio, *Description of the Ruins of an Ancient City, Discovered Near Palenque, in the Kingdom of Guatemala* (London, 1822), 46; E[dward] A[ugustus] Kendal[l], "Account of the Writing-Rock in Tauton River," *Memoirs of the American Academy of Arts and Sciences* 3 (1809): 165-91. The *Palmyra Register*, 2 June 1819, published an account of the discovery and supposed decipherment of the "Writing Rock."

44. Smith, *View of the Hebrews*, 187.

45. Yates and Moulton, 45.

46. Boudinot, 181; "American Antiquities," *Palmyra Herald*, 30 Oct. 1822.

47. Smith, *View of the Hebrews*, 103-104, 144, 164; Beatty, 91-92; Edwin James, *Account of an Expedition from Pittsburgh to the Rocky Mountains*, 2 vols. (Philadelphia, 1823), 1:268.

48. Smith, *View of the Hebrews*, 101, 108, 158.

49. Ibid., 99, 104.

50. Ibid., 98-107. Cf. Al. 11:28-29, 14:5.

51. Ibid., 98, and many others. Early Christian missionaries were quick to exploit the Indians' belief in the "Great Spirit" by associating it with the God of Christianity. See Edward Augustus Kendall, *Travels through the Northern Parts of the United States, in the Years 1807 and 1808*, 3 vols. (New York, 1809), 2:264-67. Cf. Al. 22:9-10.

52. Smith, *View of the Hebrews*, 101, 159, 163.

53. Ibid., 210-12. Cf. Mos. 15:1-5; 3 Ne. 11:36.

54. Worsley, 161-62.

55 Francesco Saverio Clavigero, *The History of Mexico*, Charles Cullen, trans., 3 vols. (Philadelphia, 1817), 2:14.

56. Rio, unpaginated and unnumbered plate near beginning of book.

57. See Howard W. Goodkind, "Lord Kingsborough Lost His Fortune Trying to Prove the Maya Were Descendants of the Ten Lost Tribes," *Biblical Archaeology Review* 11 (Sept.-Oct. 1985): 60, 65. Also Wauchope, 64-65; William H. Prescott, *History of the Conquest of Mexico*, 3 vols. (New York: Harper and Brothers, 1843), 3:384-87.

58. Jeremy Belknap, *A Discourse, Intended to Commemorate the Discovery of America* (Boston, 1792), 48.

59. [Samuel Mather], *An Attempt to Shew, that America Must be Known to the Ancients* (Boston, 1773), 22-25. Mather's book was still known and discussed in New York as late as 1814. See *The New York Magazine, and General Repository of Useful Knowledge* 1 (July 1814): 154-56.

60. Calvigero, 2:13-15.

61. Rio, 92-94, 104; Mark Beaufoy, *Mexican Illustrations* (London, 1828), 220-21; [Samuel Purchase], *Purchase His Pilgrims*, 7 vols. (London, 1625), 3:1123, 4:1219, include descriptions by Francis de Gomora and Antonie Knivet which link the legend of Quetzalcoatl with St. Thomas.

62. Boturini is quoted by Kingsborough [Edward King], *Antiquities of Mexico* (London, 1831-48), in Lynn Glaser, *Indians or Jews?* (Gilroy, CA: Roy V. Boswell, 1973), 13. See also Prescott, 3:383.

63. Smith, *View of the Hebrews*, 204-207.

64. Ibid., 205.

65. See Goodkind, 65. Also Muriel Porter Weaver, *The Aztecs, Maya, and Their Predecessors: Archaeology of Mesoamerica* (New York: Seminar Press, 1972), 204-207.

66. Samuel Sewall, *Phaenomena Quaedam Apocalyptica* (Boston, 1697), 35-36.

67. Ibid., 1-2, 42. Sewall apparently believed in an American-based New Jerusalem as early as 1684 when he discussed the subject with Cotton Mather. See Ola Elizabeth Winslow, *Samuel Sewall of Boston* (New York: Macmillan Co., 1964), 152-56. Cotton Mather discussed the American New Jerusalem in *Theopholis Americana* (Boston, 1710), 43-44, as did Nicholas Noyes in *New Englands Duty and Interest* (Boston, 1698), 74-75, 85. The establishment of the New Jerusalem in America is another important concept which the Book of Mormon shares with its Puritan background. Various aspects of this concept have been discussed in the following sources: Alan Heimert, "Puritanism, the Wilderness, and the Frontier," *The New England Quarterly* 26 (Sept. 1953): 380-82; Gustav H. Blanke and Karen Lynn, " 'God's Base of Operations': Mormon Variations on the American Sense of Mission," *Brigham Young University Studies* 20 (Fall 1979): 83-92. On 8 October 1823, the *Wayne Sentinel* reported that someone had founded a New Jerusalem in Kentucky.

68. Smith, *View of the Hebrews*, 184.

69. Ibid., 172.

70. Ibid., 172-73.

71. Belknap, 45-46.

72. DeWitt Clinton, *Discourse Delivered before the New-York Historical Society* (New York, 1812), 53.

73. Ibid., 61.

74. Yates and Moulton, 40.

75. Solomon Spalding, *The "Manuscript Found." Manuscript Story, by Rev. Solomon Spaulding, Deceased* (Liverpool: Millennial Star Office, 1910), 10-11, 18, 20-25.

76. "Indian Antiquities," *Palmyra Register*, 21 Jan. 1818, reprinted from the *North American Review and Miscellaneous Journal* (Boston) 16 (Nov. 1817): 136-37; *Palmyra Herald*, 19 Feb. 1823.
77. Smith, *View of the Hebrews*, 88, 152; Adair, 194.
78. Smith, *View of the Hebrews*, 206.
79. "Of the Aborigines of the Western Country," pt. 1, *Port Folio*, fourth series, 1 (June 1816): 458-59.
80. Ibid., 459.
81. Ibid., 461.
82. Yates and Moulton, 42-44, 46, 92.
83. Henry Home [Lord Kames], *Sketches on the History of Man*, 2 vols. (Edinburgh, 1774), 2:1, 11, 29. Kames's book was published in Philadelphia in 1776 as *Six Sketches on the History of Man*.
84. Adair, 2; see also Samuel Stanhope Smith, *An Essay on the Causes of the Variety of Complexion and Figure in the Human Species. To which are Added Strictures on Lord Kaims's Discourse, on the Original Diversity of Mankind* (Philadelphia, 1787), 27, 33. Others who shared Adair's and Smith's view that the Indians' skin color was the result of environmental and climatic conditions include Penn, *A Letter*, 5; P[ierre] de Charlevoix, *Journal of a Voyage to North-America*, 2 vols. (London, 1761), 1:15, which mentions Edward Brerewood's belief in the theory; and "Aborigines of America," pt. 2, *American Monthly Magazine* (Boston) 1 (May 1829): 82-86. Also useful in tracing the debate in America between climatic and polygenetic theories are John C. Greene, "The American Debate on the Negro's Place in Nature, 1780-1815," *Journal of the History of Ideas* 15 (June 1954): 384-96; and William H. Hudnut III, "Samuel Stanhope Smith: Enlightened Conservative," *Journal of the History of Ideas* 17 (Oct. 1956): 540-52. See also Margaret T. Hodgen, *Early Anthropology in the Sixteenth and Seventeenth Centuries* (Philadelphia: University of Pennsylvania Press, 1964), passim.
85. Adair, 4.
86. Ibid.
87. J. W. Powell, ed., *Twelfth Annual Report of the Bureau of Ethnology, 1890-1891* (Washington, D.C.: Government Printing Office, 1894), xli-xlii.
88. Jason Whitman, "The Book of Mormon," *Unitarian* (Boston), 1 Jan. 1834, 46.
89. Enos 20. The Indians' nakedness was to the Puritans a sure sign of their inherent savage nature. Edmund Burke's statement that the Europeans found the natives "quite naked, except those parts, which it is common for the most uncultivated people to conceal" was a typical sentiment (1:168). Spalding described the ancient "Delawares" in his novel: "Their clothing consisted of skins dressed with the hair on—but in warmer weather, only the middle part of their bodies were incumbered with any covering—The one half of the head of the men was shaved & painted with red" (11).
90. "To establish any connection at all between the books of the two Smiths," argued Brigham Young University religion professor Hugh Nibley in 1959, "it is absolutely imperative to find something perfectly unique and peculiar in both of them" ("The Comparative Method," *Improvement Era*, Nov. 1959, 848). The theory that the Indians were degenerates who destroyed

NOTES TO CHAPTER FOUR

their more civilized brethren rather than the prevalent theory of two distinct races constitutes, so far as can be determined, an original idea with Ethan Smith. The Book of Mormon differs with Smith regarding the ten tribes but parallels him on other features. Apparently Oliver Cowdery, Joseph's scribe, had a step-mother who attended Ethan's church in Poultney, Vermont, and may have even become acquainted with Smith himself. See Wesley P. Walters, "The Use of the Old Testament in the Book of Mormon" (M.A. thesis, Covenant Theological Seminary, 1981), 97-98, 212-14; and David Persuitte, *Joseph Smith and the Origins of the Book of Mormon* (Jefferson, NC: McFarland & Co., 1985), 5-8.

91. Recently Mormon leaders changed the Book of Mormon's promise that latter-day Indian converts will turn "white and delightsome" by insisting on an 1840 edition reading of "pure and delightsome" (*Ensign*, Oct. 1981, 17-18). The 1981 printing of the Book of Mormon follows that reading. However, the original manuscript, the printer's manuscript, the 1830 first edition, and the 1837 second edition all use the words "white and delightsome."

92. *Vermont Patriot and State Gazette* (Montpelier), 19 Sept. 1831.

93. President Ezra Stiles of Yale recorded two such instances in his diary. Under the date 16 October 1786, he wrote: "Mr. Benedict & Mr. Mudge told me there was an Indian Sam Adams . . . now living in New Lebanon, who had been growing White for now about two years. It began on his Breast & the Skinning and Whiteness has spread all over his Body, except the Extremities—& there is increasing. . . . Of three p[er]sons comparing with him, he was the whitest, clear skin, fair red & white." Under the date 5 April 1787, he wrote: "Yesterday the Rev. Mr. Ball of Amity told me that in 1757 at Setauket South on L. Isld. he saw an Indian Man grown white in spots or pyed all over. He stript off his Shirt & shewed Mr. Ball his Body. The Indian had been in Health, & Sickness was not the Cause of it. But he never heard whether the Indian became white all over or not." Franklin Bowditch Dexter, ed., *The Literary Diary of Ezra Stiles*, 3 vols. (New York: Charles Scribner's Sons, 1901), 3:243, 259.

94. A copy of the revelation, penned by W. W. Phelps to Brigham Young, 12 Aug. 1861, LDS church archives, appears in Fred C. Collier, comp., *Unpublished Revelations of the Prophets and Presidents of the Church of Jesus Christ of Latter-day Saints* (Salt Lake City: Collier's Publishing Co., 1979), 57-58; and is reprinted in Steven F. Christensen, "Scriptural Commentary," *Sunstone* (Nov.-Dec. 1981): 64. Mormon scholar Lyndon W. Cook cited the revelation and listed it as an uncanonized revelation of Joseph Smith but did not publish the text (*The Revelations of the Prophet Joseph Smith: A Historical and Biographical Commentary of the Doctrine and Covenants* [Provo, Utah: Seventy's Mission Book Store, 1981], 347, 361). Recently, Richard S. Van Wagoner noted some problems regarding the accuracy of Phelps's reminiscent account, particularly as it relates to polygamy. See his *Mormon Polygamy: A History* (Salt Lake City: Signature Books, 1986), 223-24.

Joseph Smith was not the first to suggest that white Americans intermarry with Indians. In 1816 William H. Crawford (1772-1834), senator from Georgia, made the highly controversial suggestion that Americans solve their

Indian problem by intermarrying with them (*American State Papers: Indian Affairs*, 2:28, in Chase C. Mooney, *William H. Crawford, 1772-1834* [Lexington, KY: University Press of Kentucky, 1974], 88). Mooney states that the idea of civilizing the Indians through intermarriage had been previously recommended by Patrick Henry and Thomas Jefferson and that the idea had gained some acceptance among Creek, Cherokee, and Chickasaw Indians (89, 292). When Crawford was candidate for the presidency eight years later, the issue was again brought up for debate. For a heated response to Crawford's position, see Thomas Cooper, *Strictures to James Madison on the Celebrated Report of William H. Crawford Recommending the Intermarriage of Americans with Indian Tribes* (Philadelphia, 1824). On 25 December 1824, the *Cincinnati Literary Gazette* claimed "the second generation resulting from these alliances would be totally white and beautiful."

95. Sidney B. Sperry, *Book of Mormon Compendium* (Salt Lake City: Bookcraft, 1968), 31-39.

96. The Reverend M. T. Lamb (*The Golden Bible; or, The Book of Mormon. Is It from God?* [New York: Ward and Drummond, 1887], 109) believed the Book of Mormon erred in the matter of animal sacrifice:

> According to the law of Moses the firstlings of their flocks were never offered as burnt offerings or sacrifices. All firstlings belonged to the Lord, de jure, and could not be counted as a man's personal property—whereas, all burnt offerings, or sacrifices for sin of every kind, must be selected from the man's own personal property, or be purchased with his own money for that purpose, while all firstlings of the flock, as the Lord's property, came into the hands of the high priest, and by him could be offered up as a peace offering, not as a burnt offering or a sin offering, himself and family eating the flesh. (See Ex. 13:2, 12 and 22:29, 30; Numb. 3:13; 2d Sam. 24:24; Numb. 18:15-18 and other places.)

97. For a discussion of the early Americans' interpretation of their own history, see, among others, Ernest Lee Tuveson, *Redeemer Nation: The Idea of America's Millennial Role* (Chicago: University of Chicago Press, 1968); Russel B. Nye, *This Almost Chosen People: Essays in the History of American Ideas* (East Lansing: Michigan State University Press, 1966), especially Chapter 4 on "The American Sense of Mission."

98. Robert Silverberg, *Mound Builders of Ancient America: The Archaeology of a Myth* (Greenwich, CT: New York Graphic Society, 1968), 48-49.

99. Ibid., 42-47.

100. H. M. Brackenridge to Thomas Jefferson, 25 July 1813, *Belles-Lettres Respository* (New York) 1 (1 Aug. 1819): 291-92.

101. Powell, xliii-xliv. On the demise of the mound-builder myth, see Silverberg, 166-221.

102. A general discussion of the Adena and Hopewell cultures can be found in Silverberg, 222-337. See also Gordon R. Willey, *An Introduction to American Archaeology*, 2 vols. (Englewood Cliffs, NJ: Prentice-Hall, 1966-71), especially vol. 1, *North and Middle America*; Martha A. Potter, *Ohio's Prehistoric Peoples* (Columbus: Ohio Historical Society, 1968).

NOTES TO THE CONCLUSION

1. Among those in both the LDS and RLDS churches who have publicly questioned the Book of Mormon's historicity are Wayne Ham, "Problems in Interpreting the Book of Mormon as History," *Courage: A Journal of History, Thought and Action* 1 (Sept. 1970): 15-22; William D. Russell, "A Further Inquiry into the Historicity of the Book of Mormon," *Sunstone* 7 (Sept.-Oct. 1982): 20-27; Blake Ostler, "An Interview with Sterling M. McMurrin," *Dialogue: A Journal of Mormon Thought* 17 (Spring 1984): 25-26; and George D. Smith, "Joseph Smith and the Book of Mormon," *Free Inquiry* (Winter 1983-84): 21-31. In a talk given to religious education faculty at Brigham Young University, political scientist Louis Midgley acknowledged a growing trend among some Mormons to view the Book of Mormon as "inspired fiction" and to offer "naturalistic explanations" for foundational events. This trend, Midgley feared, constituted a more sophisticated, "more subtle," and "more dangerous" threat to the Mormon faith than any previous attack by outsiders. Midgley unfortunately failed to consider seriously the challenges facing the historicity of the Book of Mormon or the strengths of a less literalistic approach. See Louis Midgley, "Some Challenges to the Foundations," 14 Sept. 1984, copy in author's possession.

2. For Mormon attempts at minimizing the significance of the 1830 material, see, for example, Hugh Nibley, "The Comparative Method," *Improvement Era* (Oct.-Nov. 1959): 744, 848, passim; and those compiled in James D. Bales, *The Book of Mormon?* (Rosemead, CA: Old Paths Book Club, 1958), 160-245. On the weakness of these attempts, especially Nibley's apologetic, see Madison U. Sowell, "The Comparative Method Reexamined," *Sunstone* 6 (May-June 1981): 44, 50-54.

3. For example, one scholar from the Reorganized Church of Jesus Christ of Latter Day Saints said it was not possible for Joseph Smith "to plagiarize [sic] from other publications the wonderful information divulged in the Book of Mormon for the simple reason that there was none; at that time American archaeological investigation had scarcely begun" (in Bales, 162). For other Mormon claims, consult Chapter 14 of Bales's book.

4. Paul R. Cheesman, *The World of the Book of Mormon* (Salt Lake City: Deseret Book Co., 1978), 78.

5. Kirk Holland Vestal and Arthur Wallace, *The Firm Foundation of Mormonism* (Los Angeles: LL Co., 1981), 106. Compare similar pronouncements in Paul R. Cheesman, "Ancient Writings in the Americas," *Brigham Young University Studies* 13 (Autumn 1972): 83-84; Hugh Nibley, *Lehi in the Desert and The World of the Jaredites* (Salt Lake City: Bookcraft, 1952), 122; Hugh Nibley, *Since Cumorah: The Book of Mormon in the Modern World* (Salt Lake City: Deseret Book Co., 1967), 251.

6. Clark Braden, *The Braden-Kelley Debate* (St. Louis: Christian Publishing Co., [1884?]), 68. Kelley incorrectly assumed that Josiah Priest's *American Antiquities* had first appeared in 1834; the first edition, however, appeared in 1833.

7. Milton R. Hunter, *Archaeology and the Book of Mormon* (Salt Lake City: Deseret Book Co., 1956), 205-6.

8. John L. Sorenson, *An Ancient American Setting for the Book of Mormon* (Salt Lake City: Deseret Book and the Foundation for Ancient Research and Mormon Studies, 1985), 87.

9. I. Woodbridge Riley, *The Founder of Mormonism: A Psychological Study of Joseph Smith, Jr.* (New York, 1902), 87.

Bibliography

The following is an annotated bibliography of select pre-1830 English and American sources dealing with the origin, history, and antiquities of the New World Indians relevant to the study of the Book of Mormon.

Entries typically include four kinds of notations. First, the book or periodical is identified according to its bibliographical information, excluding the publisher's name, and is often referenced by a shortened title. Second, the availablity of a source in a microfilm or microtext collection is included for interested readers, although this may not be comprehensive. The following abbreviations refer to microfilm sources:

ACS   *American Culture Series 1493-1875: A Cumulative Guide to the Microfilm Collection: American Culture Series I and II, Years 1-20, with Author, Title, Subject, and Reel Number Indexes.* Edited by Ophelia Y. Lo. Ann Arbor, MI: University Microfilms International, 1979. (Numbers here refer to reel and item numbers; thus ACS 075.008 means reel 75, item 8 in the American Culture Series.)

APS   *American Periodicals, 1741-1900; An Index to the Microfilm Collections: American Periodicals, 18th Century; American Periodicals, 1800-1850; American Periodicals, 1850-1900; Civil War and Reconstruction.* Edited by Jean Hoarnstra and Trudy Heath. Series 1, 2, and 3. Ann Arbor, MI: University Microfilms International, 1979. (Numbers here refer to series and reels; thus APS 2:363 means series 2, reel 363 in the American Periodical Series).

E   Charles Evans. *American Bibliography; A Chronological Dictionary of All Books, Pamphlets and Periodical Publications Printed in the United States of America, from the Genesis of Printing in 1639 Down to and Including the Year 1820.* 14 vols. [1639-1799.] New York: Peter Smith, 1941-59. Readex Microprint. Edited by Clifford K. Shipton. Worcester, MA: American Antiquarian Society. (Numbers here refer to items in collections; thus E 24086 means item 24086 of the Evans collection. Readex Microprint collection and the Evans bibliography use the same numbering system.)

LAC   *The Microbook Library of American Civilization.* Chicago: Library Resources, 1971. Author and Title Catalogs, 1971; Subject Catalog and Biblioguide, 1972. (Numbers here refer to items in collections; thus LAC 14288 means item 14288 in the Library of American Civilization.)

SAB *Bibliotheca American. A Dictionary of Books Relating to America, from Its Discovery to the Present Time.* Begun by Joseph Sabin, continued by Wilberforce Eames, and completed by R. W. G. Vail for the Bibliographical Society of America. 29 vols. New York: Sabin, 1868-1936. Reprint. Amsterdam, N. Israel, 1961-62. Microfiche collection. Louisville: Lost Cause Press, c. 1971-81. (Numbers here refer to alphabetical listings of collections; thus SAB 155 means item 155 in the bibliography.)

SS Ralph R. Shaw and Richard H. Shoemaker. *American Bibliography; A Preliminary Checklist for 1801-1819.* 19 vols. New York: Scarecrow Press, 1958-63.

———. *A Checklist of American Imprints for 1820.* New York and London: Scarecrow Press, 1964.

———. *A Checklist of American Imprints for 1821-1829.* 9 vols. Metuchen, NJ: Scarecrow Press, 1967-71. Readex Microprint for 1800-1819. Edited by John B. Hench. Worcester, MA: American Antiquarian Society. (Numbers here refer to items in collections; thus SS 24528 means item 24528 in Shaw-Shoemaker.)

W Donald Wing. *Short-Title Catalogue of Books Printed in England, Scotland, Ireland, Wales, and British America and of English Books Printed in Other Countries, 1640-1700.* 3 vols. New York: Columbia University Press, 1945-51. *Early English Books, 1641-1700: Selected from Donald Wing's SHORT TITLE CATALOGUE.* Ann Arbor, MI: University Microfilms International, 1974-78. Microfilm. (Numbers here refer to items in collections; thus W 206 means item 206 in Wing.)

If a microfilm or microtext collection uses an edition of a work other than the one cited, I have indicated so in brackets immediately following microfilm or microtext information.

Third, a list of other known pre-1830 editions of a work is given, compiled from *The National Union Catalog, Pre-1956 Imprints*, 685 vols., Supplements 686-754 (London: Mansell, 1972), Evans, Shaw-Shoemaker, and Wing. I have made no attempt to check every edition of a work and thus accept responsibility only for the edition cited in the bibliographic entry. Finally, the bibliography provides a brief summary of a source's contents as they pertain to the Book of Mormon (page numbers correspond to the edition first cited).

In compiling a working bibliography, I found the following sources especially helpful: Thomas Warren Field, *An Essay towards an Indian Bibliography. Being a Catalogue of Books, Relating to the History, Antiquities, Languages, Customs, Religion, Wars, Literature, and Origin of the American Indians, in the Library of Thomas W. Fielding* (New York, 1873); Dale L. Morgan, "Documents from Early Mormon History," John Phillip Walker, comp. (unpublished manuscript in my possession); James D. Bales, *The Book of Mormon?* (Rosemead, CA, 1958); Charles A. Shook, *Cumorah Revisited* (Cincinnati, 1910); Robert Silverberg, *Mound Builders of Ancient America:*

The Archaeology of a Myth (Greenwich, CT, 1968); Lee Eldridge Huddleston, *Origins of the American Indians: European Concepts, 1492-1729*, Latin American Monographs, no. 11 (Austin, 1967); Gustav H. Blanke, "Early Theories about the Nature and Origin of the Indians, and the Advent of Mormonism," *Amerikastudien* 25 (1980): 243-68; Ethan Smith, *View of the Hebrews; or the Tribes of Israel in America* (Poultney, VT, 1825); and Josiah Priest, *American Antiquities and Discoveries in the West* (Albany, NY, 1833).

The following bibliography together with this book demonstrate that curiosity among Joseph Smith's contemporaries about the New World and its Indians was widespread. Again, however, I wish to remind readers that the works which follow do not necessarily represent direct borrowings in regards to the text or composition of the Book of Mormon.

I. Books

Acosta, Joseph [de] (1539-c. 1600). *The Naturall and Morall Historie of the East and West Indies*. Translated by E[dward] G[rimston]. London, 1604. ACS 075.008. Originally published in Latin in 1589, in Spanish in 1590, 1591, and 1608.

> Acosta traveled to Peru as a Jesuit missionary in 1570. His book was the first to deal with problems regarding men and animals in the New World. He does not commit himself on Indian origins, except to say that he is sure they came from Adam (50-51), and is skeptical of contemporary speculations that the Indians came from Atlantis or were descendants of the ten tribes (71-77). He also rejects the notion that the Indians migrated by sea, whether intentionally or because of storms (56-71). Rather Acosta suggests that both men and animals entered the New World through a northern passage where the Old World and the New touched or were in close proximity (64-68).

Adair, James (c. 1709-c. 1783). *The History of the American Indians*. London, 1775. LAC 14288; SAB 155.

> Adair was a pioneer Indian trader who lived among the North American Indians (principally the Chicksaw and Cherokee), 1735-75. He wrote his book, a proof that the Indians descended from the ten tribes of Israel, to contradict writers such as Lord Kames who asserted the Indians were pre-Adamites (3). Adair's evidence for the Indian-Israelite theory consists of twenty-three parallels between Indian and Jewish customs. For example, he claims the Indians spoke a corrupt form of Hebrew (37-74), honored the Jewish sabbath (76), performed circumcision (136-37), and offered animal sacrifice (115-19). He also describes ancient fortifications which he had personally observed (377-78). Although Adair's thesis was later dismissed, his account of the various tribes, their customs and vocabularies, together with his narration of life among the Indians continues to interest scholars.

Adams, Hannah (1755-1832). *The History of the Jews*. 2 vols. Boston, 1812. SS 24528; LAC 22643. London, 1818.

Adams discusses the Indian-Israelite theory of Manasseh ben Israel and James Adair (2:333-38) and mentions the black Jews of Cochin and their brass plates (2:197-99).

Ashe, Th[omas] (1770-1835). *Memoirs of Mammoth, and Various Other Extraordinary and Stupendous Bones, of Incognita, or Non-Descript Animals, Found in the Vicinity of the Ohio, Wabash, Illinois, Mississippi, Osage, and Red Rivers, &c. &c.* Liverpool, 1806. SAB 2179.

———. *Travels in America*. 3 vols. London, 1808. [New York, 1808; SAB 2180.] London, 1809, 1818; Baltimore, 1808; Newburyport, MA, 1808; Pittsburgh, 1808; New York, 1808, 1811.

Irish traveler Thomas Ashe describes several ancient fortifications and burial mounds he encountered during his 1806 trip to North America (1:76-86, 308-19, 2:13-16, 26-34).

Barton, Benjamin Smith (1766-1815). *Archaeologiae Americanae Telluris Collection et Specimina; or, Collections with Specimens, for a Series of Memoirs on Certain Extinct Animals and Vegetables of North-America.* Philadelphia, 1814. SAB 3803.

Barton describes various mammoth bones found in North America.

———. *New Views of the Origin of the Tribes and Nations of America*. Philadelphia, 1797. ACS 230.003; LAC 15385; SAB 3819. Philadelphia, 1798.

Barton compares the Indian's language to several Old World languages, including the Semitic languages (80).

———. *Observations on Some Parts of Natural History*. London, [1787?]. SAB 3820.

In 1775 Barton accompanied his uncle, David Rittenhouse, to survey the western boundary of Pennsylvania. He describes the Indians and various mounds in the area. In addition, Barton rejects the notion that the Indians had Christian doctrines before their discovery (47).

Bartram, John (1699-1777). *Observations on the Inhabitants, Climate, Soil, Rivers, Productions, Animals, and Other Matters Worthy of Notice. Made by Mr. John Bartram, in His Travels from Pennsylvania to Onodago, Oswego and the Lake Ontario, In Canada.* London, 1751. ACS 013. 146; LAC 14492.

Bartram mentions the controversy over Indian origins and declares that only God knows why men have different skin colors (vii-viii).

Bartram, William (1739-1823). *Travels*. London, 1766. SAB 3870. Philadelphia, 1791; London, 1792, 1794; Dublin, 1793.

Bartram describes several ancient fortifications.

Beatty, Charles (1715?-72). *The Journal of a Two Months Tour*. London, 1768. SAB 4149. Edinburgh, 1798.

In 1755, Beatty, a Presbyterian clergyman, became chaplain to Pennsylvania troups sent to defend the northwestern borders of the state against Indians. This gave him an opportunity to observe the Indians. Beatty favors the Indian-Israelite theory and makes comparisons between Indian customs and the law of Moses (27, 83-92).

Beaufoy, Mark (1764-1827). *Mexican Illustrations*. London, 1828. SAB 4169

Beaufoy describes Mexican pyramid temples and fortifications, including the buildings at Palenque (189-99, 218), and mentions ancient hieroglyphical books (199, 221) and the theory that St. Thomas preached the gospel in ancient Mexico (150, 220-21).

Beaufoy, [Mark?]. *Tour through Parts of the United States and Canada*. London, 1828. ACS 452.004; LAC 12142; SAB 4168.

Beaufoy, a British subject, visited entrenchments and burial mounds in Ohio (104). "Some insist they are the remains of a civilized people, exterminated by the Indian hordes from Asia," he wrote. He also mentions the pyramids of Mexico and the Welsh theory of Indian origins.

Beck, Lewis C[aleb] (1798-1853). *A Gazetteer of the States of Illinois and Missouri*. Albany, 1823. SAB 4231.

Beck describes ruins of stone buildings (203, 305), mounds (43, 203, 281, 331), and mammoth bones (260).

Belknap, Jeremy (1744-98). *A Discourse, Intended to Commemorate the Discovery of America*. Boston, 1792. E 24085.

Belknap discusses the problems of Indian origins and how the gospel reached America (43-44, 48). He suspends judgment on Indian origins and rejects the notion that the gospel was preached in ancient America. He also describes fortifications in Ohio (44-45).

Bernhard, Karl (1792-1862). *Travels through North America, during the Years 1825 and 1826*. 2 vols. Philadelphia, 1828. ACS 093.003.

Bernhard describes the mammoth skeleton he saw at Peale's Museum in Philadelphia (1:139-40).

Bingly, William (1774-1823). *Travels in North America*. London, 1821. LAC 13140. London, 1823.

Bingly mentions the mammoth skeleton found in New York (4-5) and the one in Peale's Museum (48).

Bonnycastle, R[ichard] H[enry] (1791-1847). *Spanish America*. Philadelphia, 1819. London, 1818.

Bonnycastle describes ancient fortifications, temples, ruins, and highways in Mexico and Peru (55, 58-59, 70, 91-92, 99-100, 107-108, 113-16, 120-22).

Boudinot, Elias (1740-1821). *A Star in the West; or, a Humble Attempt to Discover the Long Lost Ten Tribes of Israel*. Trenton, 1816. LAC 14290; SAB 6856.

The title of this work was no doubt inspired by Claudius Buchanan's popular book, *A Star in the East* (Boston, 1811), which claimed the ten tribes were east of Israel in Persia and India. Boudinot wrote to defend the Indians' character and to save them from extinction. He relies heavily on evidences compiled by James Adair. He also mentions the Indians' lost book of God (110-11).

Brachenridge, H[enry] M[arie] (1786-1871). *Views of Louisiana*. Pittsburgh, 1814. SS 30979.

Brachenridge describes mounds and palisaded forts in North America (121, 183-88) and mentions various theories on Indian origins, including the Indian-Israelite theory of Adair (189-90).

Brerewood, Edward (1565?-1613). *Enquiries Touching the Diversity of Languages*. London, 1674. London, 1614, 1622, 1635.

Brerewood, an English philologist, believed the North American Indians to be a group of Tartar origin who came to America via the northern land bridge. He also states that animals came by the same route, for certainly no one would have transported wild and vicious beasts.

Bry, Theodore de (1528-98). *Grands Voyages*. Frankfort, 1590. ACS 003.002.

Bry's book is a collection of pieces by various authors who had described the New World and its natives.

Buchanan, James. *Sketches of the History, Manners, and Customs, of the North American Indians, with a Plan for Their Melioration*. 2 vols. New York, 1824. LAC 22210. London, 1824.

Buchanan, a British consul at New York, urges the Americans to be merciful to the Indians, who are being mistreated (1:vii-xi). He reviews various theories on Indian origins but refrains from speculating himself (1:13), reprints a speech of Samuel Jarvis arguing that Indian religion is not like Judaism as Adair and others suppose (2:1-47), and includes an "Extract from Blome's State of His Majesty's Isles and Teritories in America" [London, 1687], which states that the Indians are the lost ten tribes (2:101).

Bullock, W[illiam] (fl. 1808-28). *Six Months Residence and Travels in Mexico.* London, 1824. London, 1825.

Bullock describes Mexican temples, fortifications, and idols (111-12, 326-42).

[Burke, Edmund] (1729?-97). *An Account of the European Settlements in America.* 2 vols. 2nd ed. London, 1758. LAC 20774. London, 1757, 1758, 1760, 1765, 1766, 1770, 1777, 1808; Dublin, 1762.

Burke describes how the Indians looked when they were first discovered (1:167-75). He also mentions the Mexican and Peruvian temples (1:173) and gives an account of Montezuma receiving Cortes as the returning white god (1:70-129).

Burnet, Thomas (1635?-1715). *The Theory of the Earth: Containing an Account of the Origin of the Earth.* 2 vols. London, 1684. W 206. London, 1690, 1691, 1697.

Burnet, an early primitivist, believes the Indians reflect man's true, innocent nature (1:249) and discusses how Adam's posterity could have come to the New World after the Flood (1:270-73).

Burton, Richard [Nathaniel Crouch] (1632?-1725?). *The British Empire in America.* London, 1684. W 178. London, 1685, 1692, 1698, 1702, 1711, 1728, 1729, 1739.

Burton, an anti-primitivist, includes many examples of Indian barbarity, cruelty, idleness, and idolatry.

———. *A Journey to Jerusalem.* Philadelphia, 1794. E 26833. London, 1672; Glasgow, 1786; Hartford, 1796.

Burton discusses the ten tribe theory (31-36, passim).

Carter, Jarvis. *A Topographical Description of the State of Ohio, Indiana Territory, and Louisiana.* Boston, 1812.

Carter describes mammoth bones (48).

Carver, J[onathan] (1710-80). *Three Years Travels through the Interior Parts of North-America.* Philadelphia, 1796. LAC 13164. Philadelphia, 1784, 1786, 1789, 1792; Boston, 1794, 1797, 1802; Portsmouth, NH, 1794; Edinburgh, 1792, 1798, 1807, 1808; Glasgow, 1805; Walpole, NH, 1813.

Carver's Travels is probably the work of Dr. John Lettsome (see E. G. Bourne, "The Travels of Jonathan Carver," *American Historical Review* 11 [Jan. 1906]: 287-302). The book contains a lengthy discussion of the various theories on Indian origins (115-253) and a description of ancient fortifications (35-36).

Casas, Bartolome de las (1474-1566). *A Relation of the First Voyages and Discoveries Made by the Spaniards in America.* London, 1699. LAC 16616.

Charlevoix, P[ierre Francois Xavier] de (1682-1761). *Journal of a Voyage to North-America.* 2 vols. London, 1761. ACS 540.005.

In his thorough and scholarly "Preliminary Discourse on the Origin of the Americans" (1:1-59), Charlevoix reviews previous theories and presents his own views on the subject. He evidently believes that all men descended from Adam and that the Indian's skin color is due to climatic and environmental conditions (1:15, 47, 49). Hence he concludes that the Indians came to the New World shortly after the dispersion from the tower of Babel in a ship similar to Noah's (1:49, 53).

Chastellux, [Francois Jean] de (1734-88). *Travels in North America.* 2 vols. London, 1787. ACS 481.001. [New York, 1827; LAC 12165.] Paris, 1786; Dublin, 1787; New York, 1827, 1828.

Chastellux describes ancient entrenchments he visited in North America (1:411).

Clarke, Adam (1760?-1832). *The Holy Bible . . . with a Commentary and Critical Notes.* 6 vols. N.p., 1810. Many editions, including New York, 1811-25; London, 1810-17.

Clarke rejects the ten tribe theory of Indian origins and instead places the Israelites in Persia and vicinity (2:535-36).

Clavigero, Francesco Saverio (1731-87). *The History of Mexico.* Translated by Charles Cullen. 3 vols. Philadelphia, 1817. SS 40488. London, 1787, 1807; Philadelphia, 1804, 1817; Richmond, VA, 1806.

Clavigero describes Mexican fortifications (2:174). He discusses and rejects the notion that St. Thomas preached the gospel to the ancient Americans (2:13-15).

BIBLIOGRAPHY

Clinton, DeWitt (1769-1828). *Discourse Delivered before the New-York Historical Society.* [6 Dec. 1811]. New York, 1812.

    Clinton, governor of New York, describes the various fortifications in his state (57-58). He also makes a distinction between the mound builders and the Indians, who supposedly destroyed the mound builders in a terrible war (53, 61).

Cooper, W. D. *The History of North America.* New Brunswick, 1802. SS 2088. London, 1789; Bennington, VT, 1793, 1800; Lansingburgh, NY, 1795, 1805; New York, 1796, 1797, 1809; New Brunswick, 1797; Philadelphia, 1797, 1798; Catskill, NY, 1810, 1811; Hartford, 1814; Albany, 1815, 1818.

    Cooper, largely indebted to Edmund Burke, describes the Indian's appearance at the time of their discovery. He finds them a naked and idle people (2-3).

Cotton, John (1584-1652). *God's Promise to His Plantations.* Boston, 1634. E 402. London, 1630; Boston, 1686.

    Cotton, a leader in the New England Puritan community, justifies taking the Indians' lands by asserting that they are lazy and neglecting of God's command to subdue the earth (4-5).

Crawford, Charles (b. 1752). *An Essay upon the Propogation of the Gospel.* Philadelphia, 1799. E 35362. Philadelphia, 1801.

    Crawford believes that America was settled by two major groups: first, by descendants of Noah before the earth was divided in the days of Peleg; later, by the ten tribes (17). He cites evidence of the Indians' Hebrew origins from Adair and Penn (20-23) and urges his fellow Christians to resist conflict with one another and rather concentrate their efforts on civilizing and converting the Indians (40-48).

Cusick, David (d.c. 1840). *Sketches of the Ancient History of the Six Nations.* Lewistone, NY, 1827. [Lockport, NY, 1848; ACS 085.004].

    Cusick records Indian fables which he believes support the mound builder myth. One fable, for example, speaks of the descendants of two brothers continually at war with the other until one group is finally destroyed in North America. These fables, according to Cusick, explain the remains of fortifications and burial mounds in New York state, including those near Canandaigua (about ten miles south of the Joseph Smith, Sr., farm).

Duncan, John M. (1795?-1825). *Travels through Part of the United States and Canada in 1818 and 1819.* 2 vols. New York, 1823. ACS 100.001. Glasgow, 1823.

Duncan describes the Indian's religion and America's ancient antiquities (2:91-101). Like Clinton, he distinguishes between the mound builders, whose bodies supposedly filled the burial mounds of North America, and the Indians, who were said to have destroyed them (2:91-93).

du Pratz, [Antonoine Simon] le Page. *The History of Louisiana.* London, 1774.

Du Pratz suggests multiple origins for the American Indians. For example, he speculates that some Indians might have descended from Phoenicians or Carthaginians who shipwrecked on the shores of South America. The hieroglyphic writing of the Mexicans suggests to him that their ancestors might have been Chinese or Japanese. He also comments on the resemblance between North American Indians and the Tartars of Asia. In addition, he mentions the discovery of mammoth bones in Ohio.

[Dwight, Theodore] (1796-1866). *The Northern Traveller.* New York, 1826. New York, 1825, 1828.

Dwight describes mounds and fortifications in western New York (74, 102-3).

Dwight, Timothy (1752-1817). *Travels; in New-England and New-York.* 4 vols. New Haven, 1821-22. LAC 23194-96. [ACS 542.003; London, 1823].

Dwight, eighth president of Yale College, describes various theories on Indian origins and specifically denounces the pre-Adamite theory (1:126).

Eden, Richard. *The History of Travel in the West and East Indies.* London, 1577. ACS 002.010.

Eden discusses Indian origins and the cause of their skin color (4-5).

Edwards, Jonathan (1745-1801). *Observations on the Language of the Mahhekaneew Indians; in which . . . Some Instances of Analogy Between That and the Hebrew are Pointed Out.* New Haven, 1788. ACS 160.001. New Haven, 1787; London, 1788; New York, 1801; Boston, 1823.

Edwards argues that Indian language was derived from Hebrew.

Ellicott, Andrew (1754-1820). *The Journal of Andrew Ellicott.* Philadelphia, 1803. LAC 15198; ACS 078.006. Philadelphia, 1814.

Ellicott describes a burial mound he visited near Wheeling, West Virginia (9).

Flint, Timothy (1780-1840). *A Condensed Geography and History of the Western States for the Mississippi Valley.* 2 vols. Cincinnati, 1828. LAC 22672-73; ACS 047.006.

Flint, missionary and author of several works, describes the mounds of New York and Ohio (1:192-95). He too adopts the theory that the mounds were built by people more industrious and numerous than the Indians but rejects the notion that the mound builders used iron tools (1:193-94, 2:164, 314). He also mentions the discovery of mammoth bones in North America (1:197).

_____. *Recollections of the Last Ten Years, Passed in Occasional Residences and Journeyings in the Valley of the Mississippi.* Boston, 1826. LAC 16608.

Flint describes the Indians as savage and uncivilized (135, 156-67, 159, passim). He mentions the idea that they were Jewish but does not commit himself on the subject (136). He describes various burial mounds and fortifications of North America (157, 164-70) and mentions the discovery of mammoth bones and stone coffins (171-73). He distinguishes between mound builders and Indians (157, 164-65).

Freneau, Philip [Morin] (1752-1832). *Poems.* Philadelphia, 1796. ACS 020.204. [Philadelphia, 1772; LAC 40118.] Philadelphia, 1786, 1809; Providence, RI, 1797.

Freneau jointly composed a poem with H. H. Brackenridge, "The Rising Glory of America" (42-58). In this poem, the authors reject the pre-Adamite theory on the grounds that the Bible makes it clear that the entire world was destroyed during the Flood. Some philosophers had speculated that the Indians survived by climbing the Andes Mountains, but Freneau and Brackenridge reject the notion, arguing that the mountains were made by convulsions which accompanied the Flood (43-44). They speculate that the Indians came to America via the northern passage and were possibly descendants of the Jews, Siberians, or Tartars (44). Their poem also suggests that the New Jerusalem may be built in America (57).

Gass, Patrick (1771-1870). *A Journal of the Voyage amd Travels of a Corpse of Discovery.* Pittsburgh, 1807. LAC 12290. Pittsburgh, 1808; London, 1808; Philadelphia, 1810, 1811, 1812.

Gass describes North America's ancient fortifications, which he believes are a thousand years old (34-35).

Gomora, Francisco Lopez (1510-60?). *The Pleasant Historie of the Conquest of the West India.* London, 1578. ACS 002.009. London, 1596.

Gomora mentions that temples and towers of Mexico were made of lime stone and the houses of brick (35). He describes the great temple of Mexico and its idols (201-6).

Goodrich, Charles Augustus (1790-1862). *A History of the United States of America.* 3rd ed. Hartford, 1823. LAC 11675. Hartford, 1822, 1824, 1826; Brattleboro, VT, 1823, 1828; Bellows Falls, VT, 1824, 1825, 1826, 1827, 1828; Greenfield, MA, 1824, 1825, 1828; New York, 1824, 1825, 1826; Louisville, KY, 1825; Lexington, KY, 1827; Boston, 1827, 1828.

Goodrich includes a general discussion of Indian origins (7-19).

Gookin, Daniel (1612?-87). *Historical Collections of the Indians in New England.* Boston, 1792. Boston, 1793.

Gookin discusses the various theories of Indian origins (4).

Gordon, James Bentley (1750-1819). *An Historical and Geographical Memoir of the North-American Continent.* Dublin, 1820. ACS 423.007.

Gordon describes the mounds of Mexico (45-47).

Gordon, Thomas F. (1787-1860). *The History of Pennsylvania, from Its Discovery by Europeans to the Declaration of Independence in 1776.* Philadelphia, 1829. SAB 28002.

Gordon describes the mounds of the Mississippi valley (44).

Hakluyt, Richard (1552?-1616). *Divers Voyages Touching the Discoveries of America.* London, 1582. ACS 002.012.

_____. *Principal Navigations and Discoveries of the English Nation.* London, 1589. ACS 003.001.

Both of Hakluyt's books are collections of pieces by various authors who described the New World and its natives. They contain both early primitivist and anti-primitivist assessments of the Indians.

Hale, Matthew (1609-76). *The Primitive Origination of Mankind.* London, 1677. London, 1678, 1779.

Hale discusses the problems of animal and human origins in the Americas. He believes that their uniqueness is the result of climatic and environmental conditions and rejects the notion that Indians were products of a special act of creation (198-203).

[Hale, Sarah Josepha (Buell)] (1788-1879). *The Genius of Oblivion; and Other Original Poems.* Concord, NH, 1823.

Hale's romance depicts the mound builders of North America as coming by ship from Tyre, a hundred miles from Jerusalem, during the siege of Nebuchadnezzar of Babylonia, 585-73 B.C. She concludes her work with eight pages of notes where she describes mounds and fortifications (65-69) and mentions that some fortifications had "pickets" (69).

According to Hale, mound builders had metallurgy, including a knowledge of how to make steel (72). She believes that they were a different race than the Indians (67-68).

Hariot, Thomas (1560-1621). *A briefe and true report of the new found land of Virginia.* London, 1588. ACS 002.015. London, 1589, 1590.

Hariot includes anti-primitivist views regarding the Indians' religion and customs.

Harris, Thaddeus Mason (1768-1842). *The Journal of a Tour into the Territory Northwest of the Alleghany Mountains; Made in the Spring of the Year 1803.* Boston, 1805. LAC 13219; ACS 078.010; SAB 30515.

Harris, a Unitarian clergyman in Massachusetts, describes the burial mounds and fortifications of Ohio and elsewhere (61-63, 147-62). He speculates that the fortifications were more than a thousand years old and once included, in addition to ridges of earth, wooden walls (155, 157). He rejects the notion that the mound builders were expert metallurgists but maintains a distinction between them and the Indians (153, 160). He also mentions the discovery of ancient inscriptions and mammoth bones (178, 182).

Haywood, John (1762-1826). *The Natural and Aboriginal History of Tennessee.* Nashville, 1823. SAB 31085.

Haywood, first president of the Tennessee Antiquarian Society, attempted a pre-history of the state. He compares American antiquities with those of Hindus, Egyptians, and Hebrews. He describes North America fortifications and Mexican temples (77, 107, 121-53, 168-73) and discusses the mound builders' use of metals, including steel (11, 181 348-49), copper and brass plates (82, 345-46, 348), and metal coins (173-82, 342-43). He reports the discovery in a mound of brass plates inscribed with strange characters (82), describes stone boxes used by the Indians to bury their dead (203-4, 348, 352), discusses the possible use of the wheel and horse in ancient America (134, 163), and concludes that the mound builders were a white people destroyed by the Indians (1, 191, 218).

[Heald, Henry]. *A Western Tour, in a Series of Letters Written during a Journey through Pennsylvania, Ohio, Indiana, and into the States of Illinois and Kentucky:—Giving an Account of the Soil, Face of the Country, Antiquities and Natural Curiosities.* [Wilmington, DE, 1819?].

Heckewelder, John Gottlieb Ernestus (1743-1823). *An Account of the History, Manners, and Customs, of the Indian Nations, Who Once Inhabited Pennsylvania and Neighbouring States.* Philadelphia, 1819. ACS 160.003; LAC 15143. Philadelphia, 1818.

See the description under *Transactions of the Historical and Literary Committee of the American Philosophical Society* in the pre-1830 periodical section of this bibliography.

Herrera, Antonio de (1559-1625). *The General History of the Vast Continent and Islands of America.* Translated by John Stevens. 6 vols. London, 1740.

Herrera describes the Indians, their antiquities, and their customs.

Hobbes, Thomas (1588-1679). *Leviathan.* London, 1651. W 107. London, 1680?

Hobbes, an anti-primitivist, believes the Indians live in an inferior state of existence (I, xiii, 83).

Home, Henry [Lord Kames] (1696-1782). *Six Sketches on the History of Man.* Philadelphia, 1776. E 14801. Dublin, 1774-75, 1775, 1779; London, 1774; Edinburgh, 1778, 1807, 1813; Basil, 1796; Glasgow, 1802, 1819.

Home, a Scottish judge also known as Lord Kames, defends the idea that the American Indians descended from pre-Adamites (1, 11, 29).

Howitt, E[manuel]. *Selections from Letters Written during a Tour through the United States, In the Summer and Autumn of 1819; Illustrative of the Character of the Native Indians, and of Their Descent from the Lost Ten Tribes of Israel.* Nottingham, [1820]. SAB 33372.

Howitt describes ancient fortifications he has visited (135-6, 183). He believes the mounds were erected more than a thousand years previous (183), states that they were the work of a people superior to the Indians (136), and mentions the mound builders' use of iron (135, 183). He also subscribes to the thesis that Indians are descendants of the ten tribes of Israel (161-84). He describes the mammoth skeleton on display during his 1819 visit to Peale's Museum in Philadelphia (61).

Hubbard, William (1621-1704). *A General History of New England, from the Discovery to MDLXXX.* Boston, 1815. LAC 13230. Cambridge, MA, 1815.

Hubbard rejects the ten tribe theory of Indian origins but is certain that the Indians descended from Adam and Eve (26-27).

———. *A Narrative of the Troubles with the Indians in New England, from the First Planting Thereof in the Year 1607, to this Present Year 1677.* Boston, 1677. LAC 15306. Boston, 1775; Worcester, MA, 1801; Norwich, CT, 1802; Danbury, CT, 1803; Stockbridge, MA, 1803; Brattleboro, VT, 1814.

Hubbard states that only God knows the true origin of the Indians (1).

Humboldt, Alexander [von] (1769-1859). *Concerning the Institutions and Monuments of the Ancient Inhabitants of America.* Translated by Helen Maria Williams. London, 1814.

_____. *Personal Narrative of Travels to the Equinoctial Regions of the New Continent, during the Years 1799-1804.* Translated by Helen Maria Williams. 7 vols. London, 1818-29. SS 34971. London, 1814-29, 1818, 1822; Philadelphia, 1815.

As traveler, explorer, and scientist, Humboldt, one of the most qualified men of his day, reports to his fellow Europeans his finds in the New World. For example, he describes antiquities of North America and Mexico (6:315-22).

_____. *Political Essay on the Kingdom of New Spain.* Translated by John Black. 4 vols. London, 1811. SS 23066. [Baltimore, 1813; SS 28788.] [London, 1811-14; LAC 22213-15.] London, 1822; New York, 1811; Baltimore, 1813 [abridged edition].

Humboldt decribes Mexican fortifications and temples (1:33; 2:62-70) and mentions the use of metals in Mexico (3:111-15).

Imlay, George [Gilbert] (1754?-1828). *A Topographical Description of the Western Territory of North America.* London, 1793. ACS 103.001. [London, 1792; ACS 122.007]. London, 1797; Dublin, 1793.

Imlay includes a letter from John Hart to Benjamin Smith Barton describing North American fortifications (296-304) and an essay by John Filson, "The Discovery, Settlement, and Present State of Kentucky," which claims mound builders buried their dead in stone boxes (305-306) and describes mammoth bones found in North America (306-308).

[Irving, Washington] (1783-1859). *A History of New York . . . by Diedrich Knickerbocker.* 2nd ed. 2 vols. New York, 1812. SS 25726. New York, 1809, 1824, 1826; Philadelphia, 1819, 1829; London, 1820, 1821, 1824, 1825, 1828; Glasgow, 1821; Paris, 1824.

Among other so-called learned theories of his day, Irving pokes fun at various ideas about Indian origins, including the pre-Adamite theory (1:24-38).

Israel, Manasseh ben (1604-57). *The Hope of Israel.* Translated by Moses Wall. London, 1652. First published in Latin (Amsterdam, 1650); subsequently translated into English (1650, 1651, 1652, and 1792), Spanish (1650, 1659, 1723), Dutch (1666), Judeo-German (1691, 1712), and Hebrew (two editions before 1703, six thereafter).

Israel includes the story of Antonio de Montezinos that a remnant of the ten tribes of Israel had been discovered in the wilderness of Peru, reports the discovery of Hebrew inscriptions and Jewish synagogues in South America, and notes the similarity between certain Jewish and Indian customs. According to Israel, the discovery of the ten tribes in America was a sign that the coming of the Messiah was near.

James, Edwin (1797-1861). *An Account of an Expedition from Pittsburgh to the Rocky Mountains.* 2 vols. Philadelphia, 1823. Philadelphia, 1822, 1824; London, 1823.

James describes North American mounds and fortifications (1:59-66) and mentions the "lost races" theory to explain their existence (1:62-63). He also discusses the theory that the Indians came from Asia (1:64-65).

Jarvis, Samuel Farmer (1786-1851). *Discourse on the Religion of the Indian Tribes of North America.* New York, 1820.

In this speech delivered before the New York Historical Society on 10 December 1819, Jarvis argues for a more objective study of the Indians' religion and flatly rejects the ten tribe theory of Adair and Boudinot (8-10).

Jefferson, Thomas (1743-1826). *Notes on the State of Virginia.* Boston, 1802. London, 1787; Philadelphia, 1788, 1794, 1801, 1825; Baltimore, 1800; Walpole, NH, 1801; New York, 1801; Newark, 1801; Trenton, 1803; Boston, 1829.

Jefferson had long been interested in America's antiquities, and in his only published book, he discusses the North American mounds and the discovery of mammoth bones. He was also one of the first to study the mounds by strata and to suggest that the dead were buried at various times rather than all at once after some great war.

Jones, David (1736-1820). *A Journal of Two Visits Made to Some Nations of Indians on the West Side of the River Ohio, in the Years 1772 and 1773.* Burlington, 1774.

Jones describes ancient fortifications found in Ohio (56-57).

Juarros, Domingo (1752-1820). *A Statistical and Commercial History of the Kingdom of Guatemala.* Translated by J[ohn] Baily. London, 1823. SAB 36817. London, 1825.

Juarros claims his history of Guatemala was taken from ancient manuscripts. He rejects the pre-Adamite theory, argues the Indians originated in the Old World (118), and mentions the Indian-Israelite theory (162). According to him, the original inhabitants arrived in the New World shortly after the dispersion from the tower of Babel, since the Indians retain stories both of the tower and of the Flood (208-9). Juarros also describes Guatemalan fortifications, buildings, temples, and palaces, including the ruins of Palenque (18-19, 171-72, 187, 383).

Kalm, Pehr (1716-79). *Travels into North America.* Translated by John Reinhold Foster. 3 vols. London, 1770-71. ACS 629.005; LAC 20681-82. London, 1772.

    Kalm describes mammoth bones found in North America (1:135; 3:12).

Kendall, Edward Augustus (1776?-1842). *Travels through the Northern Parts of the United States, in the Years 1807 and 1808.* 3 vols. New York, 1809. ACS 129.003; SAB 37358; SS 17862.

    Kendall describes palisaded fortifications in North America (1:92) and Indian inscriptions found on rocks (1:241-46; 2:221-24; 3:230-31).

Ker, Henry. *Travels through the Western Interior of the United States, from the Year 1808 up to the Year 1816.* Elizabethtown, NJ, 1816. SS 37997.

    Ker discusses various theories on Indian origins (151-70), describes an ancient mound-builder city discovered in North America (324), and mentions mammoth bones (320-23).

Kilbourn, John (1787-1833). *The Ohio Gazetteer.* 6th ed. Columbus, 1819. SS 48423. Columbus, 1816, 1817, 1818, 1821, 1826, 1829; Albany, 1817.

    Kilbourn describes burial, temple, and fortification mounds in Ohio (21-25). The North American mounds commence in western New York, he writes, and extend through the western states in a southwest direction, terminating in Mexico (21).

Laskiel, George Henry. *History of the Mission of the United Brethren among the Indians in North America.* London, 1794. LAC 14030.

    Laskiel discusses various theories of Indian origins (1-2).

Lescarbot, Mark. *Nova Francia: Or the Description of that Part of New France which is One Continent with Virginia.* Translated by Pierre Erondelle. London, 1609.

    Lescarbot entertains the idea that the Indians descended from and inherited the curse of Canaan but because of his primitivist view of the Indians doubts the theory. His translator, however, believes the Canaanite theory and is consequently more harsh in his description of the Indians' character (vi, 215, 264).

L'Estrange, Hamon (1605-60). *Americans no Jewes, or Improbabilities that the Americans are of that race.* London, 1652. ACS 006.056. Probably published in 1651, though the date reads 1652.

L'Estrange, an English theologian, wrote to disprove Thomas Thorowgood's thesis that the Indians were the lost ten tribes of Israel. L'Estrange argues instead that the Indians were descendants of Noah's son Shem, who came to America at the dispersion from the tower of Babel.

[Lewis, Meriwether] (1774-1809). *History of the Expedition under the Command of Captains Lewis and Clark.* 2 vols. Philadelphia, 1814. LAC 21138-39.

This work describes ancient fortifications near the Missouri River (1:62-65).

Locke, John (1632-1704). *Two Treatises of Government.* London, 1690. W 388. London, 1694, 1698, 1713, 1728, 1764, 1772, 1824; Glasgow, 1796; Dublin, 1779

Locke was a primitivist who believed that man is better off without civilization; Indians were "natural" men still in their original and innocent state.

Loudon, Archibald. *A Selection of Some of the Most Interesting Narratives of Outrages Committed by the Indians, in Their Wars with the White People.* 2 vols. Carlisle, PA, 1811. ACS 160.006.

Loudon's description of the Indians is negative and anti-primitivist. For example, he reports idol worship and human sacrifice (2:283). However, he supports the ten tribe theory (2:285-92), mentions that the Spaniards dug up Indian tombstones covered with Hebrew characters (2:285), and compares Peruvian temples to Jewish synagogues (2:288).

Lyon, G[eorge] F[rancis] (1795-1832). *Journal of a Residence and Tour in the Republic of Mexico in the Year 1826.* London, 1828.

Lyon describes mounds and buildings in Mexico (1:54, 141, 236-42).

McCulloh, James H[aines], Jr. (1793?-1870). *Researches on America; Being an Attempt to Settle Some Points Relative to the Aborigines of America &c.* Baltimore, 1817. ACS 289.001; SS 41313. Baltimore, 1816.

McCulloh discusses various theories explaining Indian origins and also problems of transoceanic crossing (19-35). He personally favors the lost continent of Atlantis theory, popular with some of the learned but rejected by the common folk, and discusses the theory that the mound builders were a white group more advanced than the Indians (210-19).

_____. *Researches, Philosophical and Antiquarian, Concerning the Aboriginal History of America.* Baltimore, 1829. ACS 231.002.

McCulloh reviews most of the material covered in his earlier book. He describes temples in Mexico and Peru (249-371) and mounds and fortifications in North America (501-22), discusses various theories about

Indian origins, rejecting the pre-Adamite theory (418-64), mentions problems for animals migrating through the Bering Strait (428), and ultimately favors the Atlantis theory. He again discusses the theory that the mound builders were a white race far superior to the Indians (501-22).

McKenney, Thomas L[oraine] (1785-1859). *Sketches of a Tour to the Lakes.* Baltimore, 1827.

McKenney states that the origin of the Indians is unknown but believes that the time is arriving when the problem will be solved (13).

MacKenzie, Alexander (1763-1820). *Voyages from Montreal.* 2 vols. London, 1802. ACS 540.007. London, 1801; New York, 1802, 1803, 1814; Philadelphia, 1802; Baltimore, 1813.

MacKenzie describes the Chepewyan Indians of eastern North America and mentions their belief in the Flood and the long life of the patriarchs (1:145).

Martyr, Peter (1455-1526). *The Decades of the World.* London, 1812.

Martyr describes the Indians and their customs.

Mather, Cotton (1663-1728). *India Christiana. A Discourse, Delivered unto the Commissioners, for the Propagation of the Gospel among the American Indians.* Boston, 1721. ACS 374.003.

Mather supports a continuing Protestant mission to New England Indians. His description of the Indians is anti-primitivist in tone. They are "the most forlorn Ruins of Mankind, and very doleful Objects," live a life "lamentably Barbarous," and practice a religion "beyond all Expression Dark" (28). He flatly rejects the pre-Adamite theory and suggests that those in the Old World could have sailed to America (23). He also discusses the theory that the devil brought the Indians to America after Christ's resurrection in order to keep them from hearing the gospel (24) and thus rejects the notion that St. Thomas somehow preached the gospel to the ancient Americans (26).

_____. *Magnalia Christi Americana; or, The Ecclesiastical History of New-England.* 2 vols. Hartford, 1820. LAC 22361-62; SAB 46393. London, 1702

Mather includes a poem by Nicholas Noyes about Indian origins (1:14-15), mentions the ten tribe theory of Thomas Thorowgood and Manasseh ben Israel (1:506), and assesses Indian religion rather negatively (1:503-4).

_____. *The Serviceable Man.* Boston, 1690.

Mather advances the idea that the Indians migrated to America after the expulsion of the Canaanites by Joshua. The Indians—as descendants of the Canaanites and inheritors of the curse in Genesis 9:27—properly become New England's "serviceable man." It is thus God's will that the New Israel in America subjugate the Indians.

[Mather, Samuel] (1706-85). *An Attempt to Shew, that America Must Be Known to the Ancients.* Boston, 1773. E 12861; SAB 46792.

Mather, a Congregational clergyman, believes that America was populated by two major migrations, one from the tower of Babel (13) and the other, centuries later, from Asia or possibly Phoenicia (18-19). He also subscribes to the theory that ancient America was visited by Christ's apostles or perhaps by some of the seventy (22-25).

Michaux, Francois Andre (1770-1855). *Travels to the Westward of the Allegany Mountains, in the States of the Ohio, Kentucky, and Tennessee, and Return to Charlestown, through the Upper Carolinas.* Translated by B. Lambert. London, 1805. LAC 13267.

Michaux describes ancient fortifications in North America (111).

Mill, Nicholas. *History of Mexico.* London, 1824. SAB 48989.

Mill describes Mexican pyramids and compares them with those of Egypt (140, 158).

Morse, Jedidiah (1761-1826). *The American Universal Geography.* 2 vols. Boston, 1793. Philadelphia, 1793; Boston, 1796, 1802, 1805, 1812, 1829; Charlestown, 1819.

Morse, a Congregational clergyman, discusses various problems of Indian origins and rejects the pre-Adamite theory (1:75).

_____. *The History of America.* 2 vols. Philadelphia, 1808. SS 15654. Philadelphia, 1790, 1795, 1798, 1819.

Morse suggests that the Indians originally came from Asia across the Bering Strait (1:80). He mentions burial mounds and suggests that some of the larger mounds once served as bases for temples (1:98).

Morse, Jedidiah and Elijah Parish. *A Compendious History of New England.* 2nd ed. Newburyport, MA, 1809. SS 18130. Charlestown, MA, 1804, 1820; London, 1808.

Morse and Parish describe the dealings between colonists and Indians. Their interpretation of various events is typically Puritan. For example, they state that God punished the Indians with smallpox for their cruelty to the Puritan colony (20-21).

Morton, Thomas (1575-1646). *New English Canaan.* Amsterdam, 1637.

    Morton rejects the Tartar theory of Indian origins and proposes instead a Trojan origin.

[Moulton, William]. *A Concise Extract, from the Sea Journal of William Moulton.* Utica, NY, 1804. ACS 4477.002.

    Moulton describes his visits to ruined Peruvian cities with "large palaces" and "elegant buildings" and Incan highways running over a thousand miles (122, 125).

Nashe, Tho[mas]. *Christs Teares over Jerusalem.* London, 1593.

    Nashe mentions the atheistic theory that the American Indians are pre-Adamites.

Nash[e], Thomas. *Pierce Penilesse his Suplication to the Divell.* London, 1592.

    Nashe criticizes the atheistic notion that men existed before Adam.

Niles, John Milton (1787-1856). *A View of South America and Mexico.* New York, 1825. New York, 1826, 1827, 1828.

    Niles describes palaces and temples in Peru (47).

Nuttall, Thomas (1786-1859). *Journal of Travels into the Arkansa Territory, during the Year 1819.* Philadelphia, 1821. LAC 13279.

    Nuttall speaks of the destruction of ancient mound builders by the Indians (247) and describes various mounds and fortifications (25-26, 80-81, 110, 114).

Ogilby, John (1600-76). *America: Being the Latest, and Most Accurate Description of the New World.* London, 1671. W 613. London, 1670.

    Ogilby discusses various theories of Indian origins, including the ten tribe and other Hebrew theories (7-18).

Parish, Elijah (1762-1825). *A New System of Modern Geography.* Newburyport, MA, 1810. Newburyport, MA, 1812, 1814.

    Parish, a Congregational clergyman, wrote his geography for use in New England schools. He describes mounds in North America (84, 95, 100-111, 120) and the Peruvian temple at Cusco (138). He also mentions a mammoth skeleton found in South Carolina (123). Although Parish does not commit himself on any theory of Indian origins, he does include a comparison of Indian and Israelite customs (22-26).

Peale, Rembrandt (1778-1860). *Account of the Skeleton of the Mammoth.* London, 1802.

Peale discusses the mammoth skeleton which his father Charles W. Peale unearthed in 1801 in New York.

_____. *An Historical Disquisition on the Mammoth.* London, 1803.

This book is essentially a second edition of *Account of the Skeleton of the Mammoth* (1802).

[Penn, William] (1644-1718). *A Letter from William Penn.* London, 1683. ACS 008.082.

"I am ready to believe them of the Jewish Race, I mean, of the stock of the Ten tribes," wrote Penn of the Pennsylvania Indians (7). He believes their general appearance and customs are Jewish and their language similar to Hebrew (5, 7). He also believes their dark complexion the result of climatic and environmental conditions (5).

Poinsett, Joel Roberts (1779-1851). *Notes on Mexico, Made in the Autumn of 1822.* Philadelphia, 1824. London, 1825.

Poinsett mentions the Mexican tradition of the Flood (46), notes their immense pyramids and long paved roads, and mentions their hieroglyphic drawings and knowledge of astronomy and metallurgy (248).

[Priest, Josiah] (c. 1790-1850). *The Wonders of Nature and Providence, Displayed.* Albany, 1825. This book was published twice in 1825 and once in 1826. The first edition contained no plates, but the second and third editions were enlarged and included ten plates. See Winthrop Hillyer Duncan, *Josiah Priest, Historian of the American Frontier: A Study and Bibliography* (Worcester, MA, 1935), 12-15.

This work, a compilation of many previously published works, includes an extract from Francisco Clavigero's *History of Mexico* recounting the ancient Mexican traditions of idolatry and human sacrifice (569-93) and a portion from Ethan Smith's *View of the Hebrews* detailing evidence that Indians were of Hebrew origin (297-332).

Purchase, Samuel (1577?-1626). *His Pilgrimage.* London, 1613. London, 1614, 1617, 1626.

Purchase describes the New World and its inhabitants.

[Purchase, Samuel]. *Purchase His Pilgrims.* 7 vols. London, 1625.

Purchase introduces his work with an essay, "The Peopling of America" (vol. 1, bk. 1, 58-61). He also includes translations and extracts from Jose de Acosta (vol. 3, bk. 5), Bartolome de las Casas (vol. 3, bk. 5), and Antonie Knivet, who discusses the belief that St. Thomas preached the gospel in ancient America (vol. 4, bk. 6, 1219).

Rafinesque, C[onstantine] S[amuel] (1783-1840). *Ancient History, or Annals of Kentucky; with a Survey of the Ancient Monuments of North America.* Frankfort, KY, 1824. LAC 40142.

Rafinesque believes that America was populated some time after the Flood via the lost continent of Atlantis (10-13). He also mentions the discovery of mammoth bones in Ohio (9).

Ranking, John. *Historical Researches on the Conquest of Peru, Bogota, Natchez, and Talmeco, in the Thirteenth Century, by the Mongols, Accompanied with Elephants; and the Local Agreement of History and Tradition, with the Remains of Elephants and Mastodontes, Found in the New World.* London, 1827.

Ranking, inspired by Indian legends and mammoth remains, writes of thirteenth-century Mongolians who use the mammoth in their conquest of Mexico and Peru. He assumes the mound builder myth.

———. *Remarks on the Ruins at Palenque, in Guatemala, and on the Origin of the American Indians.* London, 1828.

Ranking describes the ruins at Palenque as reported by Antonio del Rio and discusses the origin of the Indians.

Rees, Abraham. *The Cyclopaedia; or, Universal Dictionary of Arts, Sciences, and Literature.* 41 vols. Philadelphia, [1805-25]. SS 9234.

According to the entry titled "America," neither Phoenicians, Carthaginians, nor Chinese came to ancient America, although Icelanders may have. The horse and the ox did not exist in America before the Spanish, but the American bison may have been used in tillage. The discovery of mammoth bones in both North and South America is also noted (vol. 1, no pagination, alphabetically arranged).

Rio, Antonio del. *Description of the Ruins of an Ancient City, Discovered Near Palenque, in the Kingdom of Guatemala.* London, 1822.

Rio describes various ruins at Palenque, including several houses and palaces and a very large building. He includes plates of some of the structures, several Mayan codices, and an article, "Teatro Critico Americano; or, a Critical Investigation and Research into the History of the Americans," written by Paul Felix Cabrera. Cabrera interprets the pre-Adamite theory of Indian origins as an attack on the atonement of Christ (28-29). He suggests instead that the ancient Americans came by sea (101). He also mentions the tradition of an eclipse in A.D. 34 and speculates that the Mexican god Quetzalcoatl was St. Thomas preaching the gospel in ancient America (93-94, 113).

Robbins, Thomas. *A View of All Religions; and the Religious Ceremonies of all Nations at the Present Day.* 3rd Ed. Hartford, 1824.

Robbins includes a section, "The Religion and Ceremonies of the North American Indians," which discusses the Indian-Israelite theory of James Adair and Elias Boudinot (158-163).

Robertson, William (1721-93). *The History of America.* 2 vols. London, 1777. LAC 20829-30. London, 1778, 1780, 1783, 1788, 1796, 1880, 1812, 1817, 1821; New York, 1798; Albany, 1822; Philadelphia, 1812, 1821, and others.

Robertson discusses various problems and theories regarding Indian origins (1:1-4), includes the stories of Cortez and Montezuma (2:1-145), of Pizarro and the conquest of Peru (2:147-266), and mentions the practice of human sacrifice in Mexican temples (2:46-47). Drawings of Mayan glyphs and a Mexican pyramid are included (483-84).

Roman, Bernard (c. 1720-84). *A Concise Natural History of East and West Florida.* 2 vols. New York, 1775. ACS 504.007; E 14440. New York, 1776.

Romans, a cartographer sent to North America by the British government, believes the Indians were a separate creation and not descended from Adam (1:38-39). Consequently, he rejects any theory which has American natives originating in the Old World, including the ten tribe theory (1:46-49). He also argues for a partial flood at the time of Noah, thus accounting for Indian survival in the New World (1:57-58).

Schoolcraft, Henry R[owe] (1793-1864). *Narrative Journal of Travels through the Northwestern Regions of the United States, Extending from Detroit through the Great Chain of American Lakes, to the Sources of the Mississippi River.* Albany, 1821. ACS 450.010; LAC 13309.

Schoolcraft mentions mounds and fortifications he saw during his travels (29-30).

Sewall, Samuel (1652-1730). *Phaenomena Quaedam Apocalyptica.* Boston, 1697. E 813. Boston, 1727.

Sewall, a Congregational clergyman, suggests that the Indians are Israelites (2, 35), that America might be the place of the New Jerusalem, and that the "other sheep" mentioned in John 10:16 are the American Indians (1-2, 42).

———. *The Selling of Joseph.* Boston, 1710.

Sewall argues against the descent of the Indians from Canaanites who were expelled by Joshua and rejexts the idea that Puritans have a right to subjugate Indians because of the curse in Gen. 9:27 (40-44).

Sigourney, Lydia Howard (1791-1865). *Traits of the Aborigines of America. A Poem.* Cambridge, MA, 1822. LAC 12069.

In her poem, Sigourney portrays the Indians in a positive light, relatively uncommon for her day, and refers to Elias Boudinot and the ten tribe theory (8-9). She appends notes to the poem defending the theory (187-88).

Simon, Barbara Anne. *Hope of Israel; Presumptive Evidence that the Aborigines of the Western Hemisphere are Descended from the Ten Missing Tribes of Israel.* London, 1829.

Smith, Ethan (1762-1849). *View of the Hebrews; or the Tribes of Israel in America.* Poultney, VT, 1825. [Poultney, VT, 1823; ACS 306.014.]

Smith's is by far the most important and interesting work dealing with the origin of the American Indians and the mound builders. Smith quotes from many other writers, both American and European, to support his thesis that the first settlers of the New World were the lost ten tribes of Israel. He also includes extracts from Alexander von Humboldt's description of Mexican antiquities, Caleb Atwater's description of the mounds and fortifications of North America, and the evidence compiled by James Adair and Elias Boudinot to connect Indians with the lost ten tribes. Smith, so far as can be determined, is the only writer before 1830 to combine the Hebrew origin theory with the mound builder myth. Several times he repeats the notion that the mound builders were destroyed by the Indians (184, 172, 173). His ten tribe theory forces him to develop the hypothesis that the Indians had degenerated from a civilized condition to their wild and savage state. He also mentions the Indian legend of the lost book of God which would one day be returned (130, 223).

Smith, John (1580-1631). *The General Historie of Virginia, New-England, and the Summer Isles.* London, 1624. London, 1625, 1626, 1627, 1632, 1666, 1727; Richmond, VA, 1819.

Smith refers to the Welsh and Carthaginian theories of Indian origins (1).

Smith, Samuel Stanhope (1750-1819). *An Essay on the Causes of the Variety of Complexion and figure in the Human Species. To which are Added Strictures on Lord Kaims's Discourse, on the Original Diversity of Mankind.* Philadelphia, 1787. LAC 12694; SAB 84103. Edinburgh, 1788; London, 1789; New Brunswick, NJ, 1810.

Smith describes the Indians as lazy and filthy and proposes that their skin color is the result of climatic conditions (27, 33). He flatly rejects Lord Kames's [Henry Home] pre-Adamite theory.

Smyth, [John] F[erdinand] D[alziel] (1745-1814). *A Tour in the United States of America.* 2 vols. London, 1784. Dublin, 1784.

Smyth mentions the mammoth bones in Ohio (1:332).

Solis, Antonio de (1679-1764). *The History of the Conquest of Mexico.* 2 vols. London, 1753.

Southey, Robert (1774-1843). *Madoc. A Poem.* 2 vols. Boston, 1806. London, 1805, 1807, 1812, 1825; Boston, 1808.

Southey's poem is based on the Welsh theory of Indian origins.

Spafford, Horatio Gates (1778-1832). *A Gazetteer of the State of New-York.* Albany, 1813. Albany, 1824.

Spafford describes various fortifications in New York (58).

Stoddard, Amos (1762-1813). *Sketches, Historical and Descriptive, of Louisiana.* Philadelphia, 1812. LAC 13321.

Stoddard discusses various theories of Indian origins (465-66) and entions the presence of white Indians in North America (474-75).

Stoddard, Solomon (1643-1729). *Question Whether God is Not Angry with the Country for Doing so Little Towards the Conversion of the Indians?* Boston, 1723. E 2479.

As the title implies, Stoddard believes that God is angry because whites have done little to convert the Indians.

Sullivan, James (1744-1808). *The History of the District of Main.* Boston, 1795. LAC 11734.

Sullivan discusses various theories of Indian origins and is satisfied with none of them (80). According to Sullivan, Ohio fortifications were built by people from Mexico and Peru because North American Indians did not possess the knowledge to construct them (83).

Thompson, George Alexander. *A New Theory of the Two Hemispheres; Whereby It Is Attempted to Explain, on Geographical Facts, the Time and Manner in which America was Peopled.* London, 1815.

Thorowgood, Tho[mas]. *Jews in America, or, Probabilities That the Americans are of that Race.* London, 1650. ACS 006.054. London, 1652.

Thorowgood includes Antonio de Montezinos's account of the discovery of the ten tribes in Peru as well as other evidence of the Israelite origin of the American Indians. He also mentions the notion that the gospel was anciently preached in America (chap. 7, 24). Thorowgood, an English theologian, emphasizes the millennialistic nature of his Indian-Israelite identification and the importance of the Indians' conversion to Christianity.

Thorowgood, Thomas and John Eliot. *Jews in America, or Probabilities, that those Indians are Judaical, made more probable by some Additionals to the former Conjecture.* London, 1660. ACS 006.064. Two editions in 1660.

Thorowgood, this time teamed with the famed "Apostle to the Indians," John Eliot of Massachusetts, strengthens his arguments that the Indians are of the ten tribes of Israel. Thorowgood had been attacked by fellow theologian Sir Hamon l'Estrange, who argued similarities listed by Thorowgood were not peculiar to Jews or Indians. Thus Thorowgood and Eliot include evidence that American Indians are distinctly Israelite.

Vega, Garcilaso de la (1539-1616). *Royal Commentaries of Peru.* London, 1688.

Vega mentions a Peruvian tradition that a race of giants built some of the great ancient buildings and that God swept them off the earth for their wickedness. Vega, a scholar, noted that horses and wheat were brought to the New World by the Spanish.

Volney, C[onstantin] F[rancois] (1757-1820). *View of the Climate and Soil of the United States of America.* London, 1804. ACS 193.002. [LAC 12704; Philadelphia, 1804].

Volney includes his essay, "General Observations on the Indians or Savages of North America" (393-491), which argues Indian skin color is the result of climatic and environmental conditions (394, 405-7). He mentions the Tartar theory of Indian origins (408) but unlike most other Indian observers, rejects the idea that all Indians look the same (411). He believes that Adair distorted and misrepresented Indian customs and language in order to prove his Indian-Israelite theory (403). He also describes the mounds and fortifications of North America as inferior to those of Mexico (485-87).

Wafer, Lionel (1660?-1705?). *A New Voyage and Description of the Isthmus of America.* London, 1699. London, 1699, 1729, 1816; Paris, 1706; Glasgow, 1794.

Wafer refers to white-skinned Indians he found in Central America (133-34).

Wakefield, Priscilla (Bell) (1751-1832). *Excursions in North America.* London, 1810. SAB 100980. [London, 1806; ACS 455.006.] London, 1806, 1819.

Wakefield visited some fortifications and saw mammoth bones at several locations along the Ohio River (115, 149).

Walton, William (1784-1857). *Present State of the Spanish Colonies.* 2 vols. London, 1810.

Walton mentions the Indian belief in the Creation and Flood (2:23-24) and includes a description of Mexican architecture and metalwork (2:43-44).

Ward, Henry George (1797-1860). *Mexico in 1827*. London, 1828.

[White, John] (1575-1648). *The Planters Plea*. London, 1630.

    White mentions the belief of some that Indians are of Ham's posterity and therefore excluded from grace until after the Jews are converted. He argues that although the Indians might be Ham's posterity, only Ham's son Canaan was cursed. The Indians, he contends, are not Canaanites (54-57).

Williams, John (1727-98). *An Enquiry into the Truth of the Tradition, concerning the Discovery of America by Prince Madog ob Owen Gwynedd, about the Year 1170*. London, 1791.

    Williams's work is based on the theory that the Indians originated in Wales.

———. *Further Observations on the Discovery of America by Prince Madog ob Owen Gwynedd, about the Year 1170*. London, 1792.

    Williams's second work is also based on the Indian-Welsh theory.

[Williams, Roger] (1604?-83). *The Bloody Tenet*. [London], 1644. W 228.

    Although Williams believes the Indians worshiped the devil, he defends their right to freedom of conscience (102-3).

Williams, R[oger]. *The Bloody Tenet Yet More Bloody*. London, 1652. ACS 006.057.

    Williams expands his previous arguments that it is unchristian to kill the Indians in order to take their lands. He argues against John Cotton's view that the Indians must be swept aside as were the ancient Canaanites to make way for God's chosen people, the Puritans. Rather, Williams insists on Puritan toleration of Indian religion: "They should be tolerated in their hideous worships of creatures and devils" (25).

Williams, Roger. *A Key into the Language of America*. London, 1643. SAB 104339. [Boston, 1827; ACS 580.010.] Boston, 1643, 1810, 1827; Charlestown, RI, 1827; also published in the *Massachusetts Historical Society Collections*, Boston, 1794, rep. 1810, 3:203-39.

    Williams believes that Indian language is a form of Hebrew and that their customs resemble those of the Jews (20-21). Although he is tolerant of the Indians, Williams believes their religion is devil inspired (112-13, 118).

Williams, Samuel (1743-1817). *The Natural and Civil History of Vermont*. Walpole, NH, 1794. LAC 11740. [Burlington, VT, 1809; SAB 104350.]

Williams discusses various theories of Indian origins, including the pre-Adamite theory, but prefers the Tartar theory (187-89). He also believes that all Indians originated from the same place (158). He mentions the discovery of mammoth bones in North America and the Indians' belief that such animals still existed in the western territories (103).

Williamson, Hugh (1735-1819). *Observations on the Climate in Different Parts of America.* New York, 1811. SAB 104451; SS 24459.

Williamson describes in detail fortifications in North America (189-99) and states that the Toltecs possessed the art of metallurgy, including the knowledge of hardening copper (113).

Wilson, J[ohn] (1588-1667). *The Day Breaking if not the Sun Rising of the Gospel with the Indians in New England.* New York, 1647. LAC 40107.

Wilson advocates a Tartar origin for the Indians (18).

Winterbotham, W[illiam] (1763-1829). *An Historical, Geographical, Commercial, and Philosophical View of the American United States, and of the European Settlements in America and the West-Indies.* 4 vols. New York, 1796. E 31647. [London, 1795; ACS 193.003.] New York, 1795; London, 1799.

Winterbotham mentions the Welsh and Carthaginian theories of Indian origins but rejects them both (1:1).

Wood, William (fl. 1629-35). *New Englands Prospect.* London, 1634. London, 1635, 1637, 1639.

Wood disagrees with those who believe the Indians spoke Hebrew (102).

Worsley, Israel (1768-1836). *A View of the American Indians.* London, 1828.

Worsley relies heavily on Ethan Smith's View of the Hebrews but adds additional information, including Manasseh ben Israel's account of Antonio de Montezinos's discovery of the ten tribes in Peru (147). Worsley believes that the tribes of Manasseh and Ephraim arrived in America first and that the other tribes followed after (150-52). He describes mounds and iron tools (137-44) and explains that the mound builders had been destroyed by the Indians (144). He also mentions the discovery of large stone crosses in Central America (161-62) and records the Indian tradition of a lost book of God (182).

Wynne, [John Huddlestone] (1743-88). *A General History of the British Empire in America.* 2 vols. London, 1770. ACS 075.007; LAC 20841-42. London, 1776.

Wynne discusses various problems of Indians coming to the New World but is certain they descended from Adam (1:19-25).

Yates, John V[an] N[ess] (1779-1839) and Joseph W[hite] Moulton (1789-1875). *History of the State of New York.* New York, 1824. LAC 15772.

Yates and Moulton trace the ancient and colonial history of New York, discussing in detail the problems and various theories of Indian origins in America (13-93). They describe mounds and fortifications in their state and neighboring states (13-20, 33-34), as well as the ruins of an ancient city near Palenque (73-77). According to them, these mounds, part of a great chain running down through Mexico and into South America (19-20), were built by a separate race of white-skinned people who were destroyed by the Indians (21-22, 40-44, 92-93). They mention the discovery of hieroglyphic writing and mammoth bones (14-15, 20), and include reports that Indians in certain locales possessed the signs and tokens of Freemasonry (55-56).

II. Periodicals

American Academy of Arts and Sciences. Memoirs. Cambridge, MA, 1785-19—. APS 2:363.

Vol. 3, 1809: E[dward] A[ugustus] Kendal[l], "Account of the Writing-Rock in Taunton River; In a letter to the Hon. John Davis, Esq. Recording Secretary of the American Academy of Arts and Sciences" discusses Indian hieroglyphic writing and includes a plate of the "Writing Rock" (165-91).

American Journal of Science (followed by *American Journal of Science and Arts*). New York, 1818-19. Edited by Benjamin Silliman. APS 2:53.

Vol. 1, 1818: Caleb Atwater, "On the Prairies and Barrens of the West . . . in letters to the Editor," discusses theories of how the North American prairies were made: one popular theory is that the aborigines burned down the forests in order to hunt wild animals, another that the forests were cut down by the aborigines in order to cultivate large crops (116). Both theories are rejected by Atwater who believes the prairies were once covered by the waters of the Great Lakes (120-24). The *Journal* also prints the call of an Ohio museum for extinct animal bones and curious works of the ancients (203-206).

American Journal of Science and Arts (follows the *American Journal of Science*). New Haven, 1820-79. Edited by Benjamin Silliman, 1818-64. APS 2:53.

Vol. 2, Nov. 1820: Caleb Atwater, "On some ancient human bones &c. with a notice of the bones of the Mastodon or Mammoth, and of various shells found in Ohio and the west," describes discovery of a mammoth skeleton by Charles W. Peale (35, 242, 245-46).

Vol. 9, June 1825: Announces that New York's Lyceum of Natural History has just received some mammoth bones (387).

Vol. 19, 1828: Reports on the mammoth skeleton at the Lyceum of Natural History in New York (31-33).

American Monthly Magazine. Boston, 1829-31. Edited by N. P. Willis. APS 2:468.

Vol 1., April-May 1829: "Aborigines of America," Parts 1 and 2, advocates the Bering Strait theory and discusses other theories of Indian origins (48-52). The article presents the idea that all American Indians are descended from the same source (45, 48) and describes Mexican idolatry, human sacrifice and "hieroglyphic paintings" (42, 44, 46). Although the Mexicans are somewhat more civilized than North American Indians, they are not the builders of the great pyramids and buildings of Central America but had assumed these from an earlier civilization (44). The article also describes North American mounds and Mexican and Peruvian structures (41-46).

Archaeologia Americana: Transactions and Collections of the American Antiquarian Society. Worcester, MA, 1820-1911.

Vol. 1, 1820: Caleb Atwater, "Description of the Antiquities Discovered in the State of Ohio and other States," describes North American mounds and fortifications, speculating that at least some of the ancient works were picketed (145), and includes several drawings of the mounds. Atwater, president of the American Antiquarian Society, believes that mound builders were metallurgists who possessed knowledge of making iron and possibly steel (232) and reports their use of "rude stone coffins" (162). At the end of this work, he offers his "Conjectures, respecting the Origin and History of the Authors of the Ancient Works in Ohio," comparing American mounds to those of various nations in Europe and Asia. He rejects the idea that the Indians or their ancestors built the mounds, thus making a sharp distinction between Indians and mound builders (206-10). The *Archaeologia* also contains a letter from Samuel L. Mitchill, professor of natural history at the University of New York, to DeWitt Clinton, president of the New York Philosophical Society, dated 31 March 1816 (325-32), which connects the Indians with Asiatics.

Belles-Lettres Repository. New York, 1819-20. Edited by A. T. Goodrich (1819) and C. S. Van Winkle (1820). APS 2:161.

Vol. 1, 1 Aug. 1819: Letter from H. M. Brackenridge to Thomas Jefferson, dated 25 July 1813, which had been read before the American Philosophical Society on 1 October 1813, reports Brackenridge's visits to mounds near Pittsburgh as well as those along the Ohio and Mississippi Rivers (290-95). He distinguishes between Indians and mound builders (291-92) and estimates that some five thousand mounds can be found in eastern North America (291).

Vol. 3, 15 May 1820: [John Haywood?], "Mounds," a reprint from the *Nashville Whig*, describes mounds near Nashville (49-52).

Vol. 3, 15 Sept. 1820: "Researches into American Antiquities" describes fortifications in Jefferson County, NY, and at Rodman, NY, (321-22).

Boston Recorder. Boston, 1817-24 (under various names, 1816-1924). Founded by Nathaniel Willis and Sidney E. Morse. APS 2:540.

Vol. 8, 27 Dec. 1823: Review of Ethan Smith's *View of the Hebrews* expresses skepticism about Smith's hypothesis and wonders if "a fertile imagination might not discover the Israelites in China or Arabia, as well as in America" (206). The reviewer also recognizes the speculative and inconclusive nature of Smith's evidence: "The time may be at hand when the origin of the Indian tribes on this continent will be clearly ascertained; but that time has not yet come" (206).

Christian Examiner and Theological Review. Boston, 1824-28 (under various names, 1813-69). Edited by John Gorham Palfrey, 1823-30. APS 2:79; LAC 31319-66.

Vol. 2, 1825: Extract from William Bullock's *Six Months' Residence and Travels in Mexico* describes Mexican temples and idols (433-34).

Cincinnati Literary Gazette. Cincinnati, 1824-25. Edited by John P. Foote. APS 2:127.

Vol. 1, 24 Jan. 1824: "The Antiquities, in the West," a satire on those who spin strange theories about North American antiquities, pokes fun at those who believed the mound builders were Christian (27).

Vol. 1, 21 Feb.-29 May 1824: C[onstantine] S[amuel] Rafinesque, "Ancient History of North America," Parts 1-6, maintains that the Indians came to America via the lost continent of Atlantis and describes mounds and fortifications of Ohio (59-60, 107-8, 116-17, 146-47, 155, 170).

Vol. 2, 25 Dec. 1824: Reviews Rafinesque's *Ancient History* and includes "Our Aborigines," an article about William H. Crawford's proposal that Americans intermarry with Indians to help civilize them as well as make their race "white and beautiful" (206-207).

Vol. 4, 2 July 1825: Contains a description and diagram of an Ohio fortification (209).

Collections of the Massachusetts Historical Society. Boston, 1792-19—. LAC 23621.

Vol. 1, 1792: Contains the entire text of Daniel Gookin's *Historical Collections of the Indians in New England* (1792).

Vol. 3, 1794: Contains the text of Roger Williams's *A Key into the Language of America* (1794).

Vol. 4, 1795: Jacob Bailey, "Observations and Conjectures on the Antiquities of America," describes North American fortifications and mentions hieroglyphic writing discovered on rocks in North America and on cloth in Mexico (100-105). He speculates that the mound builders' destruction occurred ten or twelve hundred years before the discovery of their earth works.

Columbian Historian. New Richmond, Ohio, 1824-25. APS 2:95.

Vol. 1, 13 May 1824: Discusses the problems of when and how early man reached America, favoring the opinion that both men and animals crossed the Bering Strait from Asia some time after the Flood (1-7).

Vol. 1, 17 June 1824: Exhorts readers to have faith in God's power to cause men and animals to migrate from the Old to the New World (9).

Vol. 1, 13 Aug. 1824: "Antiquities of the People who formerly inhabited the Western Parts of the United States" describes several fortifications and states that they are the work of "a people far more civilized than our Indians" (60).

Vol. 1, 20 Aug. 1824: States that mounds in North, Central and South America have a common origin (65) and mentions the mound builders' use of metals, including a purported discovery of an oxidized iron sword in an Ohio mound (65-66).

Vol. 1, 3 Sept. 1824: Describes the contents of the various North American mounds, mentions the discovery of gold, silver, copper, oxidized iron, and speculates on the existence of steel (83, 86).

Columbian Magazine, or Monthly Miscellany. Philadelphia, 1786-90. APS 1:11.

Vol. 1, Sept. 1786: "An Account of the Vices peculiar to the Savages of N[orth] America" argues against primitivist European writers who only mention Indian virtues; it lists instead Indian vices: uncleanness, nastiness, drunkenness, gluttony, treachery, idleness, and theft (9).

Vol. 1, Nov. 1786: "Description of Bones, &c. found near the River Ohio" describes mammoth bones and includes drawings of a bone, a tooth, and a tusk (105-107).

Vol. 1, April 1787: Thomas Jefferson discusses the American mammoth (366-69).

Vol. 1, May 1787: J[ohn] Heart, "Account of some Remains of ancient Works, on the Muskingum, with a Plan of those Works," describes Ohio fortifications and includes a diagram (425-27).

Vol. 1, July 1787: Gives a brief discussion on several theories about the origin of the Indians (552).

Vol. 2, May 1788: Contains "Extracts from Du Pratz's History of Louisiana, and other Authors, respecting the resemblance between the traditions and Customs of the Nations of America, and those of the Ancient Jews" (240-41). Extracts were also included in June and July issues.

Vol. 2, July 1788: Reprints John Smith's letter about Hebrew among the Indians and Charlevoix's *Journal of Travels in North America* (1761), which states Indians are similar to Jews (367-71).

Vol. 2, Nov. 1788: Contains information on fortifications at Muskingum, Ohio (645-46).

Vol. 3, Sept. 1789: Abraham G. Steiner, "Account of some Old Indian Works, on Huron River, with a Plan of them, taken the 28th of May, 1789," describes fortifications and includes a diagram (543-44).

Companion and Weekly Miscellany. Baltimore, 1804-6. Edited by Edward Easy. APS 2:13.

Vol. 1, 23 Feb. 1805: Connects the Indians with the Tartars of Asia who supposedly invaded America and destroyed the mound builders (133-34).

Gleaner; or, Monthly Magazine. Lancaster, PA, 1808-9. Edited by Stacy Potts. APS 2:32.

Vol. 1, April 1809: Contains a review and discussion of Robert Southey's poem *Madoc* (1806) which is based on the Welsh-Indian theory (355-58).

Missouri Gazette and Public Advertiser. St. Louis., 1808-22. Edited by Joseph Charles, 1808-20.

16 June 1819: Discusses Welsh-Indian theory and discovery of white Indians.

23 June 1819: Continues discussion of Welsh-Indian theory.

Monthly Review. London, 1749-1844.

Vol. 8 (second series), May 1792: Reviews Robert Ingram's edition of Manasseh ben Israel's *The Hope of Israel* (London, 1792). The review mistakenly attributes to Ingram the belief that the Jews were scattered to America after the Babylonian captivity rather than the Assyrian captivity (11).

Museum of Foreign Literature and Science. Philadelphia, 1822-42. Edited by Robert Walsh, Jr., Eliakim and Squier Littell.

Vol. 7, 1825: Compares Mexican and Egyptian antiquities (165-70). The writer knows of the works of Bullock and Del Rio.

Vol. 13, 1828: Reviews Worsley's *A View of the American Indians* (757-58). The reviewer is also aware of the works of Elias Boudinot and Ethan Smith.

Nashville Whig. Nashville, 1812-19—.

    Vol. 6, 30 May 1818: "The Mammoth" describes North American mammoth bones and reports on the Indian belief that the creature still exists.

    Vol. 7, 12 Dec. 1818: "Antiquity," reprinted from the *St. Louis Enquirer*, describes the discovery of ancient stone coffins near the Merrimack River.

    Vol. 8, 26 April 1820: [John] H[aywood?], "Mounds," describes certain mounds.

    Vol. 8, 5 July 1820: J[ohn] H[aywood], "Antiquities of Tennessee," describes mounds and ancient stone coffins found in Tennessee.

    Vol. 9, 3 Oct. 1820: "Antiquities" describes an ancient fortification discovered in Alabama.

New-Magazine, and General Repository of Useful Knowledge. New York, 1814. Edited by James Hardie. APS 2:162.

    Vol. 1, July 1814: Refers to Mather's *An Attempt to Shew, that America Must Be Known to the Ancients* (1773) and marshals additional support for his hypothesis (154-56).

New York Magazine; or Literary Repository. New York, 1790-97. APS 1:21.

    Vol. 4, Jan. 1793: "Newly Discovered Indian Fortifications" describes fortifications discovered in New York (23-24).

    Vol. 4, Oct. 1793: "Consequences of the Discovery of America and the Indians" states that many authors have tried to solve the mystery of the Indians' origin, but nothing certain has been found (582-84).

    Vol. 2 (new series), 1797: Contains a diagram of the fortification at Muskingum, Ohio (555).

Niles' Weekly Register. (*Weekly Register*, 1811-14; *Niles' Weekly Register*, 1814-37; *Niles' National Register*, 1837-49.) Baltimore, 1811-49. Edited by Hezekiah Niles. LAC 31236-62.

    Vol. 1, 11 Jan. 1812: James Foster, "American Antiquities," describes fortifications in Ohio as well as an ancient stone wall and ruins of an ancient city and its streets (360). Foster speculates that the mounds were the work of another race "much more civilized than the present Indian inhabitants." He speculates that the Indians came from Asia and are probably Scythians.

    Vol. 10, 30 March 1816: "Remains of ancient Fortifications" describes several fortifications in western New York, claiming they were surrounded by a ditch and perhaps "picketted" (68).

    Vol. 10, 15 June 1816: "American Antiquities" discusses various theories regarding the mounds (258-59).

Vol. 12, 14 June 1817: Announces the discovery of the remains of a mammoth in Orange County, New York (251).

Vol. 12, 5 July 1817: "Ancient Fortifications and Tumuli" reports on a fortification and burial mound in Ridgeway, New York (300).

Vol. 13, 27 Sept. 1817: States that the mound builders, a highly civilized nation, were destroyed by the savage Indians (74). As evidence of the mound builders' superiority over the Indians, the author claims that glass objects have been discovered in some of the mounds (74-75).

Vol. 13, 17 Jan. 1818: Reports a St. Louis paper's claim that living mammoths were seen near the Rocky Mountains (344).

Vol. 14, 13 June 1818: Reports several old Indians seeing a mammoth (279-80).

Vol. 16 (supplement), 1819: Reprints a letter from H. M. Brackenridge to Thomas Jefferson, dated 25 July 1813, which had been read before the American Philosophical Society on 1 October 1813 (89-91). The same letter was printed 1 August 1819 in the *Belles-Lettres Repository, and Monthly Magazine*. This issue of the *Register* also contains a notice that a mammoth was discovered in New York and laments that such a beast had become extinct in America, for "with teams of mammoths forests might be torn up by the roots, rocks removed, and in short, agriculture could be carried on upon a scale commensurate with the vastness of our country" (104).

Vol. 19, 28 Oct. 1820: "Antiquities, in Albama" describes mounds and fortifications discovered in Alabama (144).

Vol. 22, 10 Aug. 1822: Reports discovery of a mound in Chautauque County, New York, containing many skeletons and weapons of war (379).

Vol. 29, 3 Sept. 1825: Describes mammoth bones discovered in Genessee County, New York (6).

Vol. 32, 7 July 1827: "Mexican Antiquities" describes the Mexican antiquities, including hieroglyphic books (311).

Vol. 35, 17 Jan. 1829: Mentions mammoth bones and teeth discovered in North and South America (344).

North American Review and Miscellaneous Journal. Boston, 1815-77. Edited by William Tudor. APS 2:178.

Vol. 15, Sept. 1817: William Cullen Bryant's poem "Thanatopsis" is thought to be about the "millions" of ancient mound builders who slumber in American mounds (338-40).

Vol. 16, Nov. 1817: "Indian Antiquities" reports on an item in the *Western Gazetteer* describing several mounds found in Harrison, Indiana. The editor of the *North American Review* introduces the item by stating that the mounds were the work of a people "who had made much greater advances in the arts of civilized life" than any of the Indians (137). The article quotes a portion from the *Western Gazetteer* to the effect that the mound builders were more civilized than the Indians and that the numerous skeletons which filled the mounds "were doubtless killed in battle, and hastily buried" (137). The *Gazetteer* also mentions the discovery of several stone houses (138).

Palmyra Herald (follows *Palmyra Register*, then as *Western Farmer*, 1821-22, and followed by *Wayne Sentinel*). Palmyra, NY, 1821-23. Edited by Timothy C. Strong.

Vol. 2, 24 July 1822: Includes "Poetical Description of the Mammoth, by a Shawnee Indian."

Vol. 2, 21 Aug. 1822: "Antiquary" reports discovery of a mound containing many bones and relics near Fredonia, Chautauque County, New York.

Vol. 2, 30 Oct. 1822: "American Antiquities" reports the discovery in an Ohio mound of large skeletons buried in a Christian manner, west to east. This source also makes a distinction between mound builders and Indians.

Vol. 2, 19 Feb. 1823: Distinguishes between mound builders and Indians. The first settlers of North America are supposedly the descendants of Shem who come by sea. Later the descendants of Japheth cross the sea and subjugate them. This source also speaks of mammoths.

Palmyra Register (followed by *Western Farmer*, then *Palmyra Herald*). Palmyra, NY, 1817-21. Edited by Timothy C. Strong.

Vol. 1, 21 Jan. 1818: "Indian Antiquities" is a reprint of an article from the *North American Review* (Vol. 16, Nov. 1817) which in turn reported on an item from the *Western Gazetteer* describing several mounds found in Harrison, Indiana. The editor of the *North American Review* introduces the item by stating that the mounds were the work of a people "who had made much greater advances in the arts of civilized life" than any of the Indians. The *Western Gazetteer* is quoted as stating that the mound builders were more civilized than the Indians and that the numerous skeletons which fill the mounds "were doubtless killed in battle, and hastily buried." The *Gazetteer* also mentions the discovery of a number of stone houses. See also *North American Review*.

Vol. 1, 18 Aug. 1818: Describes a Roman coin found in Tennessee, which had caused some to speculate that the Romans built the fortifications.

Vol. 2, 26 May 1819: "American Antiquities" reports on the discovery of mounds and expresses the belief that their builders were exterminated by the Indians.

Plough Boy. Albany, 1819-23. Edited by Henry Homespun, Jr. [Solomon Southwick]. APS 2:19091.

Vol. 1, 11 Sept. 1819: "Antiquities of Marietta" reports the discovery of a sword in one of the Ohio mounds. "Here then is conclusive evidence that a people formerly inhabited the country who must have made considerable proficiency in the arts, with which the present natives were found totally unacquainted when Europeans first came among them. What has become of this people?" (118)

Port Folio. Philadelphia, 1801-27. Edited by Oliver Oldschool [Joseph Dennie]. APS: 2:40-2, 220, 228, 915; LAC 31440-84.

Vol. 4 (new series), 7 Nov. 1807: Describes Charles W. Peale's Museum in Philadelphia (293-96). Peale's Mammoth Room contained an entire mammoth skeleton which had been discovered in New York in 1801 and several other bones of prehistoric animals (295-96).

Vol. 1 (second series), Jan. 1809: Reviews Thomas Ashe's *Travels in America* (150-62) and discusses North American fortifications (159-60).

Vol. 3 (second series), Feb. 1810: Discusses mammoths discovered in the Arctic in 1806 (111-13).

Vol. 4 (second series), Oct. 1810: Letter from Benjamin Smith Barton to Thomas Jefferson, 13 July 1810, discusses the American mammoth (340-44).

Vol. 7 (second series), June 1812: Reviews Benjamin Smith Barton's *New Views of the Origin of the Tribes and Nations of America* (Philadelphia, 1797), discussing Barton's view that the Indians came from Asia. The review maintains that another race, predating but surpassing the Indians, constructed the ancient forts and cities east of the Mississippi River (507-26).

Vol. 5 (third series), Jan. 1815: Announces that the periodical possesses an unpublished manuscript which refutes the theory that America was peopled from Asia through the Bering Strait and that a portion of the manuscript will be printed in a forthcoming issue (80-81).

Vol. 5 (third series), March 1815: "Proposed Solution of the Question, Touching the Peopling of the Continent of America," an extract from the unpublished manuscript in the periodical's possession, argues the impossibility of men and animals crossing the Bering Strait, since no one would transport snakes or wolves. Rather the Pacific and Atlantic Oceans were once dry land, allowing men and animals to migrate to the New World. This land disappeared during the convulsions of the earth at the time of Peleg (231-41).

Vol. 6 (third series), July 1815: "Whence come the Men and Animals to America?" (7-10), another extract from the unpublished manuscript, again argues that animals such as iguanas, alligators, monkeys, and parrots could not have migrated through the extremely cold Arctic region.

Vol. 1 (fourth series), June 1816: "Of the Aborigines of the Western Country" reveals that the extracts published in the March and July issues, supposedly the work of Henry Frost, were in fact written by the late Dr. John P. Campbell (457). The periodical then discusses at length the common notion that the mounds and fortifications were built by a civilized, agricultural, white-skinned race. This white-skinned race, according to the *Port Folio*, came from Asia and were perhaps Israelites of the ten tribes. These civilized people were eventually destroyed by other more savage and dark-complected Asiatics who also migrated to the New World (457-63).

Vol. 2 (fourth series), July 1816: Continues the June article about the aborigines of the western country, discussing the mound builders' metallurgy and use of copper, brass, and iron (1-8).

Vol. 3 (fourth series), May 1817: Samuel Mitchill, "American Antiquities," discusses the Tartar origin of the Indians (422).

Vol. 4 (fourth series), Aug. 1817: "Origin of the North American Indians" mentions that a cross was found around the neck of a skeleton taken from a mound at Chilicothe, Ohio (168).

Vol. 4 (fourth series), Sept. 1817: C. W. Short, "Antiquities of Ohio," describes a fortification in Hamilton County, Ohio, and includes a diagram (179-81).

Vol. 7 (fourth series), April 1819: "Antiquities of the West" describes antiquities of Tennessee, including a stone fort, some glass, and an iron sword (350).

Vol. 2 (fifth series), Aug. 1822: Describes an Ohio mound, states that the mounds cannot be the work of the Indians, and compares the mounds to the pyramids of Egypt (125-26).

Portico. Baltimore, 1816-18. Edited by Tobias Watkins. APS 2:192.

Vol. 5, April-June 1818: Describes bones of a mammoth discovered in New York (311-12).

Royal American Magazine, or Universal Repository of Instruction and Amusement. Boston, 1774-75. Edited by Isaiah Thomas. APS 1:26.

Sept. 1774: Discusses mammoth bones discovered in Ohio and concludes that the species is now extinct despite stories among the Indians (349-50).

Susquehanna Register (as *Montrose Register*, 1826; *Susquehanna Register*, 1827-31?; *Susquehanna Register and Northern Farmer*). Montrose, PA, 1826-55?

18 Jan. 1826: States that "the Indians—aborigines of America—are, with a few Tartar exceptions, the literal descendants of Abraham, Isaac, and Jacob" (3).

Transactions of the Historical and Literary Committee of the American Philosophical Society. Philadelphia, 1819-43.

Vol. 1, 1819: John Heckewelder, "An Account of the History, Manners, and Customs, of the Indian Nations, Who Once Inhabited Pennsylvania and the Neighbouring States," describes ancient fortifications in the Great Lakes region (30). Heckewelder was a missionary to the Delaware Indians.

Transactions of the Literary and Philosophical Society of New York. New York. APS 2:840; SS 35116.

Vol. 2, 1815-25: DeWitt Clinton, "A Memoir on the Antiquities of the Western parts of the State of New-York," describes mounds and fortifications scattered throughout the state of New York, including those of Canandaigua and Oxford (71-84). This speech was delivered before the society on 13 November 1817.

United States Literary Gazette. Boston, 1825-26. Edited by James G. Carter. APS 2:242.

Vol. 1, 15 June 1824: Announces the discovery of a mammoth skeleton in New Jersey. The skeleton, nearly entire, was taken to New York's Lyceum of Natural History (77).

Vol. 1, 1 Oct. 1824: Reviews Ethan Smith's *View of the Hebrews* (1823). The reviewer does not agree with Smith's hypothesis that the Indians are the lost ten tribes (179-81).

Vol. 1, 15 Jan. 1825: Reviews James Buchanan's *Sketches* (1824) (292-94). In addition, the periodical also mentions various theories on Indian origins, expresses doubt that any ancient record would ever be discovered to solve the mystery, and states that the mounds and fortifications were built by a people superior to the Indians who had been driven southward and probably became the Mexicans and Peruvians.

Utica Christian Repository. Utica, NY, 1822-26. APS 2:245.

Vol. 4, May 1825: Reviews Ethan Smith's *View of the Hebrews* (143-49). The reviewer advises Smith to separate his evidence for Indian-Israelite origins into that which is strictly Hebrew and that which might be construed as patriarchal.

Wayne Sentinel (follows *Palmyra Herald*). Palmyra, NY, 1823-19—. Edited by E. B. Grandin and Pomeroy Tucker.

Vol. 2, 3 Nov. 1824: Edmund James, "Antiquities in Missouri," reports on the discovery in Missouri of an inscribed rock and ancient city and speculates that the inscriptions and city were the work of a race exterminated by the Indians.

Vol. 3, 4 Oct. 1825: Contains the speech of Mordecai M. Noah delivered at the dedication of the City of Ararat (situated on Grand Island in the Niagara River) as a refuge for world Jewry.

Vol. 3, 11 Oct. 1825: Noah, whose speech is concluded in this issue, claims that the Indians are the lost ten tribes of Israel and disputes the idea that the natives are indigenous. He also argues against the idea that the Indians are savages or inherently uncivilized.

Vol. 4, 1 June 1827: "Decyphering of Hieroglyphics" compares Mexican hieroglyphics and Egyptian hieroglyphics.

Vol. 6, 24 July 1829: Mentions a mammoth bone in New York City and reprints an item from the Batavia People's Press on "The Aborigines." This item describes the mound builders, whose once great nation "stretched from the Atlantic to the Pacific," and wonders what calamity swept them from the face of the earth, speculating that perhaps they had become so wicked that "the Almighty in his wrath utterly annihilated them."

Western Farmer (follows *Palmyra Register*, and is followed by *Palmyra Herald*, 1821-23, then by the *Wayne Sentinel*). Palmyra, NY, 1821-22. Edited by Timothy C. Strong.

Vol. 1, 18 July 1821: "A Curiosity" mentions the Indians' use of hieroglyphic-like picture writing.

Vol. 1, 19 Sept. 1821: Mentions that workers on the Erie Canal discovered human skeletons and "several plates of brass."

Western Review. Lexington, KY, 1819-21. APS 2:253.

Vol. 1, Sept. 1819: Reviews John Heckewelder's *An Account of the History, Manners, and Customs, of the Indian Nations* (65-74) and describes several Ohio mounds, explaining that it was a widespread belief that they contain the bodies of those killed in some terrible war (96-98).

Vol. 1, Oct. 1818: Reviews Francisco Clavigero's *The History of Mexico* (129-42) and describes North American mounds (171-82).

Vol. 1, Nov. 1819: Concludes the review of Calivero's book (193-202) and describes additional ruins and fortifications (193, 220-28).

Vol. 1, Jan. 1820-Vol. 2, April 1820: Two articles describe North American antiquities (346-53, 29-42, 112-20, 153-60).

Vol. 2, May 1820: Describes two ancient modes of burial which indicate to the writer that "there were too [two] powerful nations contending for the country" (200). The fortifications and burial mounds are evidence that a terrible war had been fought in North America (200). The writer also rejects the Bering Strait theory and proposes instead that the ancient Americans came by ship (204).

Vol. 3, Sept. 1820: Reviews the first volume of *Archaeologia Americana* (Worcester, MA, 1820) (89-112).

Scriptural References

Genesis
1:28—55
4:9-15—50
9:20-27—50
10:8—50
11:8—39

Matthew
28:19-20—60

John
3:14—61
10:16—61

Colossians
1:23—60

2 Esdras
13:40-41—40
13:41—44

1 Nephi
1:2—67
1:4—51
4:9—33
5:10-22—67
6:2—35
12:19—53
12:23—66, 67
13:10-12—68
13:13-24—68
13:14—68
13:17-18—68
13:30—68
13:30-32—68
13:38—68
13:40—49
13-14—6
16:10—51
16:18—33
17:17—51
17:51—35, 51
18:1-2—51
18:8—35
18:9-22—51

2 Nephi
1:10-11—68
2:20—49
5:14—33
5:15—33
5:16—31
5:16-17—21
5:17—67
5:21—66
5:24—67
9:21—49
10:11—68
25:7-8—3
25:8—5
25:24-30—67
26:22—5
28:8—6
30:6—66
31:3—3

Enos
11-18—68
20—53, 66

Jarom
5—67
8—33

Mosiah
2:3—67
8:8—21, 50
8:10-11—33
11:8—31
11:9—31
11:12—31
22:6—31

Alma
1:4—6
2:38—32
3:4—66
13—67
16:11—32
22:28—30, 51
22:30—50
22:30-31—30
22:32—51
28:11—32
39-42—6
45:10-11—53
48:8—31
49:4—31
50:1-5—32
53:3-4—32
53:7—21
62:20-23—31

Helaman
3:3-6—30
3:4—30, 67
13:18—11

3 Nephi
2:15—66
11-26—67
15:5—67
15:21-24—67
16:1-3—50
17:4—50
20:15-22—67
21:22-25—67

Mormon
2:28-29—30
2-5—30
3:20—49
4:14—67
4:21—67
5:15—66
6:4—67
8:12—11
8:14—11
9:32—67
9:32-34—67
11:6—32

Ether
1:33—35, 49
1:34-37—49
1-2—50
2:1—50
2:2-3—50
2:3—50
2:5—50
2:15—32
6:4-11—50
6:7—50
6:12—49
6:18—50
7:6—30
7:9—33
8:9—50
8:15—50
8:20—6

8:23-26—5, 6
9:18—50
9:19—50
10:23-27—33
13:1-12—67
13:2—49

Moroni
9:9-10—66

Doctrine and Covenants
3:19-20—68
20:11—49

Abraham
1:21-27—50

Index

Abdey, Edward Strut: Book of Mormon history of mound builders, 32
Adair, James: *History of the American Indians*, 41, 57; describes metal plates, 18; rejects pre-Adamite theory, 41-42, 64; ten tribe theory, 41-42, 57; weakness of methodology, 42, 57; human sacrifice, 54; Indians' skin color, 64-65
Adena culture (Indian), 69
American Monthly Magazine: South, Central, and North American antiquities described, 23; mound builders commence in the south, 28, 46
animals, 46; horse, 46; mammoth, 46-47
anti-Mormons: explanations of the Book of Mormon, 4
Archaeologia Americana: stone boxes, 18; fortifications, 25; metal objects found in mounds, 29
archaeology: early nineteenth-century beginnings, 7
Atwater, Caleb: "Descriptions of the Antiquities Discovered in the State of Ohio and Other Western States," 25; Ohio mounds described, 25-26; metal objects found in mounds, 29; letter to Nauvoo postmaster, 83n20, 84n49

Bales, James D.: *The Book of Mormon?*, 4
Beaman, Alvah: a rodsman and member of money-digging company, 13
Beaufoy, Mark: Mayan antiquities described, 23
Belknap, Jeremy: Indian origins debate, 47; doubts gospel preached in ancient America, 59-60; mound builders destroyed by Indians, 62-63
Bering Strait, 7, 46
Berkhofer, Robert F., Jr.: "Indian" as unitary concept, 8
Blanke, Gustav H.: "Early Theories About the Nature and Origin of the Indians, and the Advent of Mormonism," 4
Book of Mormon: as actual history, 3; environmental explanations of, 3, 4, 5; historical criticism of, 4-5; freemasonry reflected in, 5; Catholicism reflected in, 5-6; Universalism reflected in 6; events surrounding the coming forth of, 13-15; method used in translating, 16; mounds and fortifications described in, 31-32; Jaredite and Nephite metallurgy, 33; history of mound builders, early Mormon belief in, 30-31, 65; solves Indian origin mystery, 35, 49; supports notion of universal flood, 49; transmits early nineteenth-century errors about indigenous animals, 50; forges reconciliation of tower of Babel and ten tribes theories, 50-51; Jaredites as Hamites, 50; answers skepticism about sea travel, 51; reflects mound builder myth, 65; explains Indians' skin color, 66; stereotypes Indians, 66; Indian character described, 67; Hebrew and Egyptian

languages used by Nephites, 67; law of Moses kept in, 67; Christ's visit to America described, 67; early American history prophesied, 67-68; justifies taking Indian lands, 68; purpose of, 68; *see also* Jaredites; Nephites

Boturini, Chevalier: Quetzalcoatl as Christ, 60

Boudinot, Elias: did not visit Palmyra, New York, 90*n*41; *A Star in the West*, 42; ten tribe theory, 42

Brackenridge, Henry M., 24

Brattleboro Messenger: Book of Mormon explains mounds, 30

Bridgman, Peter G.: swears out warrant against Joseph Smith, 12

Brodie, Fawn M.: *No Man Knows My History*, 4; environmental influence on Book of Mormon, 4; fatal blow to Spalding theory, 4; *View of the Hebrews*, 42

Bullock, William: Mayan antiquities described, 23

Burke, Edmund, 55

Cabrera, Paul: rejects pre-Adamite theory, 38

Campbell, Alexander: critique of Book of Mormon, 3

Catholicism: reflected in Book of Mormon, 5-6

Charlevoix, Pierre de: *Journal of a Voyage to North-America*, 45; rejects pre-Adamite theory, 45; Indians came by sea, 45

Chase, Willard: Joseph Smith's early money digging, 14

Christianity: in ancient America, 59-60; Jeremy Belknap doubts its presence in ancient America, 60

Clavigero, Francesco: *The History of Mexico*, 87*n*15; rejects preAdamite theory, 37; human sacrifice, 54-55; Christianity in ancient America, 60; doubts Quetzalcoatl is St. Thomas, 60

Clinton, DeWitt: burial mounds described, 26; New York fortifications described, 26; metal tools used to construct mounds, 28; calculates ages of mounds, 29; mound builders destroyed by Indians, 63

Cotton, John: justifies taking Indian lands, 55

compass, 45, 51

Cowdery, Oliver: preaches to Indians, 11; describes Joseph Smith's obtaining plates, 14-15

del Rio, Antonio: *Description of the Ruins of an Ancient City*, 23; Mayan antiquities described, 23, 38; ancient American crosses, 59

deseret (honey bee), 50, 93*n*94

du Pratz, Antonoine: *History of Louisiana*, 46; ancients shipwrecked on coast of South America, 46

Dwight, Timothy: rejects pre-Adamite theory, 38-39

Edwards, Jonathan: Indians' language like Hebrew, 41, 58; *Observations on the Language of the Mahhekaneew Indians*, 58

elephants, 46-47

Eliot, John, 22, 41; *see also* Thorowgood, Thomas

Esdras: passage quoted, 40; "where never mankind dwelt," 40, 44, 92*n*93

INDEX 149

Flood: Indian belief in 37, 87*n*16; universal in Book of Mormon, 49
Freemasonry: reflected in Book of Mormon, 5

Geography: mound builder settlement compared with Book of Mormon, 30-31; limited region theory, 85*n*68; Central America as Book of Mormon's "neck of land," 86*n*73
Grandin, Egbert B.: Book of Mormon's publisher, 11

Hale, Sarah Josepha: *Traits of American Life*, 17; eighteenthcentury American money digging, 17, 79*n*30
Hall, James: *Legends of the West*, 16; early nineteenth-century American money digging, 17, 79*n*29
Harris, Martin: describes money-digging company, 13, 15; controversial letter, 14, 78*n*17; Joseph Smith's method of translation, 16
Harris, Thaddeus Mason: describes gold plates, 18; describes North American mounds, 24, 25, 26; argues mound builders had no metal tools, 28, 29
Haywood, John: stone boxes, 18; metal plates, 18; describes Mayan antiquities, 23; steel and iron objects found in mounds, 29
historical criticism, 4
Home, Henry: pre-Adamite theory, 37; *Sketches of the History of Man*, 64; Indians' skin color proves not from Adam, 64
Hopewell culture (Indian), 69
horse, 46
Howe, E. D.: *Mormonism Unvailed*, 4; *see also* Spaulding theory
Humboldt, Alexander von: *Political Essay on the Kingdom of New Spain*, 23; describes Olmec and Mayan antiquities, 23; missionaries distort Indian religion, 58
Hunter, Milton R.: argues Joseph Smith could not have known about white Indians, 72

Inca, 22; antiquities describes, 22
Indians (Americans): early nineteenth-century discussions of, 7, 8; "Indian" as unitary concept, 8, 9; Mormon missionaries visit, 11; graves of, 18; lost book of, 18-19, 48; not expert metallurgists, 29; language like Hebrew, 41, 58; location of first settlement, 45-46; character as seen by French Jesuits, 5354; character as seen by Puritans, 54-55; human sacrifice, 54-55; alcohol abuse, 55; vices, 55; idleness, 55; as savages, 55-56; character defended by Ethan Smith, 56-57; customs compared to Israelites, 57-58; glyphs like Egyptian, 59; believe in law of Moses, 58; elements of Christianity in religion, 59; skin color, 64-65, 66; Adena and Hopewell cultures, 69; nakedness of sign of savage nature, 98*n*89; cases of some turning white, 99*n*93; Joseph Smith's belief of how Indians will become white, 66, 99*n*94; *see also* origin of Indians
Israel, Manasseh ben: Incan ruins described, 21-22; ten tribe theory, 40-41; millennialism, 41

Jaredites: from tower of Babel, 8, 49-50; advanced metallurgists, 33; as Hamites, 50; Lamb questions account of sea voyage, 93*n*95
Jarvis, Samuel: rejects ten tribe theory, 57-58
Jefferson, Thomas: believed mammoths alive, 47; skeletons in mounds, 69
Juarros, Domingo: describes Mayan antiquities, 23

Kames, Lord: *see* Home, Henry
Kelley, E. L.: claims no knowledge of Mayan ruins before 1834, 71
Kinderhook plates, 93*n*96

Lamb, M. T.: questions Book of Mormon's account of Jaredite sea voyage, 93*n*95; questions Book of Mormon's account of Nephite animal sacrifice, 100*n*96
La Peyrere, Isaac de: *Theological System upon the Presupposition that Men were before Adam*, 36; pre-Adamite theory, 36
Lawrence, Samuel: seer and member of money-digging company, 13
L'Estrange, Hamon: tower of Babel theory, 39, 43; *Americans No Jewes*, 43
lost Indian book, 18-19, 48
lost tribes: *see* ten lost tribes; origin of Indians
Lumnius, Joannes Fredericus: *De Extremo Dei Judicio et indorum vocatione*, 40; ten tribe theory, 40

McCulloh, James: Atlantian theory, 45; arrival of Indians by sea rejected, 45
Mack, Solomon: fought Indians, 9
Madison, James: early rejection of mound builder myth, 68
magic: Joseph Smith's involvement, 12-13, 77*n*7; Lucy Smith admits family's involvement, 13; elements reflected in initial account of obtaining plates, 13-15; Willard Chase testimony, 14; elements reflected in Book of Mormon translation, 16
mammoth, 46-47
Marks, David: Book of Mormon contains history of mound builders, 32
Marlow, Christopher: pre-Adamite theory, 36
Mars: moons of, 6-7
Mather, Cotton: pre-Adamites theory rejected, 38; *Magnalia Christi Americana*, 48, 54; negative estimation of Indians, 54; *India Christiana*, 54
Mather, Samuel: *An Attempt to Shew that America Must Be Known to the Ancients*, 44; two migrations to New World, 44; believes gospel preached in ancient America, 60
Maya, 21; antiquities described, 23
Mernitz, Susan Curtis: "Palmyra Revisited: A Look at Early Nineteenth Century and the Book of Mormon," 4
metallurgy: mound builder, 28-29; Jaredite-Nephite, 33
money digging: Joseph Smith's involvement, 12; Joseph Smith member of money-digging company, 12, 13, 15; slippery treasures, 13; eighteenth and early nineteenth century, 16-17; in Indian mounds, 17
Mongolians: Indian origins, 7, 51, 72

INDEX 151

Montezinos, Antonio de: ten tribes in South America, 40
Morse, Jedidiah: *History of America*, 24; temple mounds, 24; *American Universal Geography*, 86n3; rejects pre-Adamite theory, 35, 38; Indians' route to New World, 44
Moulton, Joseph: *see* Yates, John
Moulton, William: *A Concise Extract, from the Sea Journal*, 22; describes Incan antiquities, 22
mound builders, 28, 29; commence in south and move northward, 28, 84n49; metallurgy, 28-29; antiquities compared with Book of Mormon, 30-31; destroyed by Indians in North America, 62-63; as same race as Indians, 62; as different race than Indians, 62-63; white-skinned, 64; Christians, 59-61, 68; demise of mound builder myth, 65, 69, 72
mounds: Joseph Smith's interest in, 17; target for money diggers, 17; stone boxes in, 18; plates in, 18; eighteenth and early nineteenth century descriptions, 24-26; burial mounds, 2425; temple mounds, 24; fortifications, 25-26; near Smith farm, 26-27; form a chain built by one group, 27-28; most remarkable in western New York, 28; nineteenth century guesses at ages, 29; described in Book of Mormon, 31-32

Nashe, Thomas: pre-Adamite theory, 36
Neely, Albert: Joseph Smith tried before, 13
New Jerusalem: to be built in America, 61
Nephites: kept law of Moses, 67; knowledge of Hebrew and Egyptian languages, 67; metallurgists, 33; white skin, 66; Christ visits, 67
Noah, Mordecai M., 90n45; ten tribe theory, 43; Indians not savages, 56

origin of Indians: some in nineteenth century correctly guessed, 7; Mongolian origin, 7, 51, 72; theological significance of discovery, 7; Book of Mormon pertains to, 11; pre-Adamite theory, 35-39; Carthaginian theory, 39; Welsh theory, 39; Atlantian theory, 39; tower of Babel theory, 39; various Jewish theories, 39, 88n29; ten tribe theory, 39-43; mode and route of travel to New World, 44-45; difficulty of migration through arctic zone, 45, 91n57; location of first landing, 45-46; Bering Strait theory, 44-45; sea travel, 45; matter unsettled without records, 47-49
Ostler, Blake T.: theory of Book of Mormon translation, 5

Palmyra, New York: in 1820s, 9; Eric Canal, 9; population, 9; newspapers and book stores, 9; library 9
Palmyra Herald: temple mounds, 24; two migrations to New World, 44, 45; Indians came by sea, 45; North America settled first, 46; mammoth, 47; mound builder myth, 63
Palmyra Register, 9; mound builder myth, 63
Paracelsus: *see* Theophrastus, Philippus
Parish, Elijah: describes Incan antiquities, 22
Peale, Charles W.: excavated and reconstructed mammoth skeleton, 46
Pearce, Roy Harvey, 55
Penn, William: ten tribe theory, 41

Phelps, William W.: mystery of Indian origins answered by Book of Mormon, 35, 44, 49
plates: Book of Mormon, 12, 13-15, 80*n*47; discovered in American mounds, 18; Old World descriptions, 80*n*47; Mormon claims, 71
Port Folio: describes plates, 18; steel and iron objects found in mounds, 29; mound builders white, 64
Powell, J. W.: demise of mound builder myth, 65, 69
Pratt, Parley P.: mystery of Indian origins solved by Book of Mormon, 35, 49
pre-Adamites, 35-39; *see also* origin of Indians
Priest, Josiah, 90*n*43; *Wonders of Nature*, 42; *American Antiquities*, 43; ten tribe theory, 43

Quetzalcoatl: as St. Thomas, 60; as Christ, 60; as Moses and Aaron, 60-61; like Christ in Book of Mormon, 67

Ranking, John: describes Mayan antiquities, 23; mammoth, 47
Rigdon, Sidney: and Spalding theory, 4; *see also* Spalding theory
Riley, I. Woodbridge: *The Founder of Mormonism*, 4; environmental influence on Book of Mormon, 4, 73
Ritchie, William A.: dates Canandaigua mound, 29
Roberts, B. H.: theory of Book of Mormon translation, 5; environmental influence on Book of Mormon 9
Rogan, John: discovers plates in stone boxes, 18
Romans, Bernard: pre-Adamite theory, 36-37

seer stone: Joseph Smith's use: to find treasures, 13; to find Book of Mormon plates, 14; to translate Book of Mormon 16; Sally Chase uses, 16; use in nineteenth century, 16-17
Sewall, Samuel: ten tribe theory, 41; Indians as "other sheep," 61; New Jerusalem to be built in America, 61
Smith, Asael: mounds near, 27
Smith, Ethan: possible influence on Book of Mormon, 76*n*16, 98*n*90; *View of the Hebrews*, 9, 42, 43, 76*n*16, 81*n*50; lost Indian book, 18-19, 48; describes North American mounds, 24; temple mounds, 24; metal in mounds dissolved by rust, 28; some metal objects found, 29; calculates ages of mounds, 29; ten tribe theory, 42; Indians' route to New World, 45; Pittsfield parchments, 48; Indians not savages, 56-57; America's duty to Indians, 56-57; Christianity in ancient America, 59; Quetzalcoatl as Moses and Aaron, 60-61; mound builders destroyed in North America, 62; mound builders same race as Indians, 62; Indians' skin color, 64
Smith, Joseph: founding prophet, 3; translator of Book of Mormon, 3; letter to John Wentworth describing Book of Mormon, 8; influence of ancestors, 9; involvement with folk magic, 12-13; use of seer stone, 13-14, 16; member of money-digging company, 12, 13, 15; 1826 trial, 13; events surrounding discovery of plates, 13-15; describes ancient Americans to family, 15; interest in Indian treasures and mounds, 17-18; mounds near father's farm, 26-27; *see also* magic, money digging, and seer stone

Smith, Lucy: Smith family involvement with magic, 12-13; Joseph describes ancient Americans to family, 15
Smith, Samuel, 11
Smith, Samuel Stanhope: rejects pre-Adamite theory, 37, 64
Smith, Silas: mounds near, 27
Smithsonian Institution, 18, 65, 69
Spalding, Solomon: origin of Book of Mormon, 4; fatal blow to Spalding theory, 4; found parchments in mound, 19; describes fortifications, 26; mentions horse and mammoth, 46, 47; mound builder myth, 63
Spalding theory: origin of Book of Mormon, 4; Riley and Brodie doubt, 4; introduced through E. D. Howe's book, 4, 75n3
Squier, Ephraim G.: *Antiquities of the State of New York*, 24
steel: *see* metallurgy
stone: *see* seer stone
stone box: Book of Mormon plates found in, 12, 14; early nineteenth century descriptions, 18; in Oxford, New York, 27; Mormon claims, 71
Stowell, Josiah: seeks Joseph Smith's help, 12; Joseph Smith works for, 12; testifies in Joseph Smith's behalf, 13; visiting Smiths when Joseph got the plates, 13
Susquehanna Register: Indian-Israelite theory, 43
Swift, Jonathan: *Gulliver's Travels*, 6

Tanner, Jerald and Sandra: *Mormonism: Shadow or Reality?*, 4
Tartars, 7
ten lost tribes theory, 39-43; *see also* origin of Indians
Theophrastus, Philippus: pre-Adamite theory, 36
Thomas, Mark: "Revival Language in the Book of Mormon," 4
Thompson, Charles: Book of Mormon as history of mound builders, 33
Thompson, Jonathan: describes Joseph Smith's method of money digging, 13
Thorowgood, Thomas: *Jews in America*, 41, 43; describes Incan antiquities, 22; ten tribe theory, 41
Turner, Orsamus: describes metal plates, 18

Unitarian: critique of Book of Mormon, 3, 32, 65
United States Literary Gazette, 48
Universalism: reflected in Book of Mormon, 6
Utica Christian Repository: reviews Ethan Smith's book, 43

vacuum domicilium, 55, 68, 95n17
Vermont Patriot and State Gazette: the Book of Mormon answers Indian origin mystery, 49; Book of Mormon explains Indians' skin color, 66

Wayne Sentinel, 9, 43; seer stones and buried treasures, 16-17; advertises Yate's and Moulton's book, 42-43; Mordecia M. Noah's speech, 43
Wentworth, John: Joseph Smith's letter to, 8
Whitmer, David: describes Joseph Smith's method of translation, 16

Williams, Roger: Indians' language like Hebrew, 41, 58; negative estimation of Indians, 54; *A Key into the Language of America*, 58

Yates, John and Joseph Moulton: *History of the State of New York*, 9, 23, 42, 47, 59; elements of Christianity in Indian religion, 59; mound builder myth, 63; mound builders white, 64